TRADE UNIONS, INFLATION AND PRODUCTIVITY

Trade Unions, Inflation and Productivity

PAOLO SYLOS-LABINI
Translated from the Italian by
ELIZABETH HENDERSON

SAXON HOUSE | LEXINGTON BOOKS

First published as Sindacati, Inflazione e Produttività
by Gius. Laterza & Figli, Rome
© Paolo Sylos-Labini, 1972

English Translation © D. C. Heath Ltd., 1974

Published by

SAXON HOUSE, D. C. Heath Ltd.
Westmead, Farnborough, Hants., England

Jointly with

LEXINGTON BOOKS, D. C. Heath & Co.
Lexington, Mass., U.S.A.

Printed in Great Britain
by Unwin Brothers Limited
The Gresham Press, Old Woking, Surrey.

ISBN 0 347 01051 2
Library of Congress Catalog Card Number 74-7641

Contents

v

Foreword

This book deal with problems of economic analysis and problems of economic policy. It gives more space to the former, and so it might be well, in the Foreword, to reverse the proportions and dwell at greater length on policy problems.

Analytical problems are discussed mainly, but not solely, in the first two chapters.

An econometric model of the Italian economy is presented in Chapter 1. With its help, an attempt is made to establish certain fundamental links between macro-economic analysis of the Keynesian type and the analysis of relative prices. Price variations necessarily entail changes in the distributive shares via a mechanism which has much in common with those described by the classical economists; in turn, changes in the distributive shares, together with variations in the components of effective demand, influence investment, or as the classics say, the process of accumulation. In the Postscript to Chapter 1 ('Historical change and econometric models') I go on to discuss an updated version of the model, prepared by Dr Carlo Del Monte, with particular reference to the most important adjustments which proved necessary when the period of observation was extended. Some of these adjustments are subjective in the sense that they express some new point of view on the part of the observer; others are objective in so far as they correspond to 'historical changes' in the economy under observation. The distinction is methodologically important, because it is a common failing of econometricians to assume implicitly that the economic system they study never changes in the course of time.

In Chapter 2 ('Market Forms, Trade Unions and Inflation') the preceding analysis of price and wage movements is taken further, in depth and breadth. An attempt is made to explain changes in different categories of prices and in industrial wages not only in the short run, as in the econometric model, but also in the long run. The short-period analysis is concerned with annual changes and is relevant in an explanation of the business cycle; the long-period analysis deals with changes over several years and is relevant in an explanation of economic growth. The theoretical discussion is supplemented by empirical data from Italy and the United States.

Chapters 3 and 4 ('Structural Inflation and Incomes Policy' and 'Investment, Productivity and Financial Policy') deal with problems both of economic analysis and of economic policy, with special reference to Italy. It is to these two chapters that the following comments apply more specifically.

In recent years a number of questions have engaged the urgent attention of economists, trade unions and politicians alike. These questions are the following: whether an incomes policy is expedient and, if so, feasible; whether the wage rises obtained by Italian workers during the three years 1969 to 1971 did anything to push up prices; whether there has been a shift in the distribution of income in favour of wage and salary earners, and if so, what consequences it had on economic growth; and whether public expenditure, monetary and credit policy contributed to current economic difficulties.

It is my hope that the last two chapters of this book may prove helpful in the quest for considered and critical answers to these questions, answers, that is, that owe nothing to preconceived ideas and emotional preferences.

Very briefly, my answer to the first question is: no, there is no case for an incomes policy, nor is it feasible in its proper sense – that is, as a policy designed to regulate wages and salaries as well as prices according to some pre-established pattern. What is needed, on the other hand, is a determined effort to introduce a different kind of economic policy based on a mechanism of systematic consultation between government and trade unions in the context of what is usually called economic planning. What is more, these consultations must not encompass merely changes in wages and prices, nor indeed stop short at general economic policy, but should extend to social policy, or what in Italy is called reform policy. There can be no certainty that such an effort will succeed; past experience is by no means encouraging. Nor can there be any certainty that even if such a mechanism can be set up, economic growth will then proceed without disturbances and setbacks. Personally, I can conceive of no economic policy capable of eliminating the roots of existing disturbances. But it should be possible, though difficult, to mitigate the bitterness and hardships involved in the uneven and troubled process of growth. This, I suggest, can be done by a gradual but radical change in our economic system, to be brought about through political struggles and economic policy itself, and ending up in a shift of the balance of power to the benefit of the working classes.

Equally briefly, my reply to the second question is: yes, the conspicuous wage rises of the years 1969 to 1971 did contribute to price increases, and this can be proved — to the extent that econometric analysis can provide any kind of proof at all. However, the crux of the matter lies not in saying yes or no, but in discovering why and how. First of all, and in general terms, it is a fact that a certain amount of inflationary pressure is innate in the very organisation of the modern capitalist economy, with its giant corporations and powerful trade unions in the leading sectors of production, not to speak of a variety of strong international pressures driving up both prices and wages. Secondly, and with special reference to what happened in Italy in recent years, it is a fact that after the 1964 investment slump many more firms urgently put through internal rationalisation schemes, in an attempt to reduce mounting labour costs by more intensive working schedules and extra shifts; it is highly likely that this exacerbated the workers' resentments until they exploded in the 'hot autumn' of 1969. Other resentments built up over the years as a result of the delaying tactics of the ruling classes in putting into effect reforms universally recognised as necessary.

We come to the third question — whether there has been a shift in the distribution of income in favour of wage and salary earners. The answer is in the affirmative, and there is reason to believe that, at least up to a point, it is a more than transitory shift. However, the profit share declined much more than would correspond to the increased share of wage and salary earners, the difference being accounted for by the higher rent of real estate property and by earnings and costs in retail trade. In industry, the profit fall had two consequences. One of them was that the private sector's industrial investment suffered a setback while, over the years, industrial investment by public enterprises and state-controlled companies expanded at a quickening pace. Secondly, as self-financing resources dwindled, credit — both for the short and the long term — became more and more important as a source of finance. (It must be stressed that falling profits are not peculiar to Italy, nor are other developments like inflation and its recently mounting rate, increasing union militancy and steeply rising wages.)

And finally, there remains the question about monetary and credit policy and public expenditure, or more generally, financial policy. Has financial policy become more important in Italy than it used to be, and have major errors been committed? The answer, again, is in the affirmative, but in a particular sense. The general view is that the government and the monetary authorities (but expecially the former) in the last few years erred on the side of loosening the purse strings too much. In my view, as I try to prove in Chapter 4, the real error most often was excessive stringency. I suggest that more should have been spent, naturally with priority for investment over consumption expenditure, though in some years even a proportionately higher increase in consumption spending would have been better than the general containment of all expenditure. However, in the last three years public expenditure grew much faster than revenue, and the deficit of the public administration in the broadest sense (central government, local authorities and other public institutions) assumed alarming proportions. Inflation admittedly is due mainly to other causes, but the public deficit has been contributing to it, especially in those areas of the economy which are particularly exposed to demand inflation (agricultural commodities and the products of the food industry). Furthermore, the public deficit puts a strain on and also creates serious distortions in the capital and credit market. Finally, it contributes to the balance-of-payments deficit, because liquidity created on behalf of the Treasury tends to escape from the circuits of liquidity created to finance production and hence can more easily be used for speculation and clandestine capital exports.

The recession in Italy during the years 1964 to 1967 was followed by a recovery which was weak and hesitating especially in industry, the spearhead of economic growth. In these circumstances the government should have stepped up not only public investment in the strict sense, but also investment by industrial firms belonging to the public sector. The government did nothing of the kind, mainly so as to avoid state-controlled companies competing with private ones in the capital market. It was not until after 1967 that Italy's economic policy makers reversed their attitude, and since then they have been encouraging the expansion of public enterprises as a prop to the economy as a whole. There can be no doubt that the 1970–72 recession would have been much worse without the compensatory effect of public-enterprise investment. But while the expansion of public enterprises, both in absolute and in relative terms, did much to help along economic recovery and growth, it also created new economic and political problems.

Increased trade union militancy (especially in 1969 and 1970), the profit squeeze (mainly in 1963 and 1964 and then again in 1970 and 1971), errors in financial policy and, finally, a variety of international influences (upward pressure on prices and wages, the oil crisis, as well as serious disturbances in the mechanism of international payments – all these contributed to Italy's present economic difficulties. But every cloud has a silver lining. True, there is a danger today that the economic situation may go from bad to worse and the political climate deteriorate; but there is also a real hope of great strides forward in the process of economic growth, as well as in the process of civic and political development.

It is encouraging that the unions' new strategy seems to give priority not to mere wage claims but to the conquest of increasing influence on economic policy. More generally, by their vigorous, sometimes disorderly and contradictory, action the working classes did much to create the current difficulties, but they also prepared the ground for a forward leap. We cannot be certain that the political parties of the left and the trade unions, who interpret and, up to a point, guide the grassroots reactions of the labour movement, will be shrewd enough to take advantage of the new situation in order to give Italy's future the imprint of socialism. We cannot be certain that this will happen. But we do know that it cannot happen without the necessary, though not sufficient, condition of critical appraisal of the forces in play and of the objective trends at work in recent years.

Paolo Sylos-Labini
Rome, 20 December 1973

The four chapters of this book are a more or less extensively revised and updated version of four articles published in four years (1967 to 1971). All of them were part of one single research programme, which ultimately goes back to some of the major theoretical propositions developed in my book *Oligopolio e progresso tecnico*, first published in Italy in 1956 and subsequently, in a translation by Elizabeth Henderson, in English under the title *Oligopoly and Technical Progress* (Harvard University Press 1962, revised edition 1969). Three of these four papers made up a book entitled *Sindacati, inflazione e produttività*, published by Laterza, Bari, in 1972 and awarded the Siglienti prize in the spring of 1973.

The first chapter of the present book ('An Econometric Model of the Italian Economy') is based on a paper originally presented at a seminar organised by the Italian National Research Council's study group on the economic problems of development, technical progress and income distribution, and subsequently published, in an English translation by Mrs Clare Spaventa, under the title 'Prices, distribution and investment in Italy, 1951–1966: an interpretation' in *Banca nazionale del lavoro Quarterly Review*, December 1967. The econometric model is used in the following chapters as a basis for an analysis of the movements of prices, wages and investment. Chapter 2 ('Market Forms, Trade Unions and Inflation') is a revised version of a paper submitted in June 1970 to an international conference on inflation, held by the Institute for Economic Research of Queen's University, Kingston, on Lake Ontario; after Professor

Neil Swan had kindly corrected my own original English text, the paper was published in 1971 by the Industrial Relations Centre of Queen's University in the Proceedings of that conference, under the title *Inflation and the Canadian Experience*. Chapter 3 ('Structural Inflation and Incomes Policy') started life as a memorandum submitted in November 1965 to a scientific meeting of the *Società italiana degli economisti* and published by it in a volume of Proceedings entitled *Prezzi e produttività*, Turin 1969; since then the paper has been drastically overhauled and also updated. Chapter 4 ('Investment, Productivity and Financial Policy') is a translation of an article published in *Note economiche*, June 1971.

I have many debts of gratitude to acknowledge, and it is a pleasure to do so. The model in Chapter 1 owes much to Dr Elio Ugonotto, whose help is acknowledged separately at the appropriate place; as regards the chapter as a whole, I am grateful for suggestions and criticism by Professors Giorgio Fuà, Pierangelo Garegnani, Augusto Graziani, Siro Lombardini, Luigi Pasinetti and Luigi Spaventa, as also by Salvatore Biasco, Luca Meldolesi, Franco Momigliano, Mauro Ridolfi, Alessandro Roncaglia, Andrea Saba, Michele Salvati, Fernando Vianello and Enrico Zaghini. A number of improvements were introduced in the original text of Chapters 2 and 4 in response to criticism and suggestions by Professors Paolo Baffi and Michele Salvati, and in Chapter 4 also as a result of conversations with Federico Caffé, Lucio Izzo, Francesco Masera, Tommaso Padoa Schioppa, Antonio Pedone and Luigi Spaventa. To all of them I express my gratitude, and specifically exonerate them of any responsibility for such errors as I may have committed in interpreting their views.

Finally, I am indebted to the publishers of *Banca nazionale del lavoro Quarterly Review* and of *Note economiche*, to the Industrial Relations Centre of Queen's University and to the President of the *Società italiana degli economisti* for permission to reproduce or use the articles and papers which make up this volume.

Chapters 3 and 4 have not previously appeared in English; they have been translated by Mrs Elizabeth Henderson, who also revised and edited the existing English texts of Chapters 1 and 2 for the purposes of this volume, and took care of my additions and amendments thereto.

P.S.-L.

1 An Econometric Model of the Italian Economy

The first part of this chapter is devoted to the theoretical hypotheses which underlie a model of the Italian economy illustrated in the second part.

My main concern has been to clarify certain theoretical points and, particularly, to initiate a type of analysis which considers variations in certain important aggregates and in certain categories of prices and wages simultaneously − which helps, in a word, to throw a bridge between macro- and micro-economics.

I Theoretical aspects

1 Price determination and price variations

Traditional analysis, based as it is on the equalisation of marginal cost on the one hand and price or marginal revenue on the other, is concerned with the problem of the determination of individual prices and gives us hardly any information on the problem of price changes. These are either dealt with by referring to shifts of demand and supply curves or treated by empirical analyses, whose theoretical foundations are usually very rudimentary and almost never in accordance with the teachings of traditional theory, even if their authors are not always aware of this fact.

Here I intend to put forward some theoretical propositions which allow a highly simplified treatment of both problems − that of price determination and that of price variations. I shall almost exclusively consider short-term changes and leave aside, barring a few remarks, the long-term variations.

I shall distinguish four sectors in the economy: (1) agriculture, (2) industry, (3) retail trade, (4) housing. The structure of the market and the price mechanisms are significantly different in the four sectors.

2 Agricultural prices: determination and short-term variations

We can assume that competitive conditions prevail in agriculture and that, therefore, price variations in the short period depend on changes in demand and supply. It must be remembered at the outset that prices supported by public authorities cannot fall below a given level.

In competitive conditions changes on the cost side affect prices only in the relatively long period. If, at given demand, cost rises, owing for instance to an increase in factor prices, the less efficient firms are gradually pushed out of the market and the ensuing fall in the level of output makes prices rise; but this final effect is achieved only by a roundabout and time-consuming process. If, instead, cost falls, owing for instance to the adoption of new production methods by some firms, product prices remain unchanged at first, then decline gradually to the extent to which the progressive firms expand their output and new firms enter the market, attracted by the higher than ordinary profits that can be obtained there.

It follows that, in competitive conditions, prices tend to equal costs only in the long run. In the short period we can expect little or no correspondence between changes in cost and changes in prices.[1]

The dependence of price changes on supply and demand in the short period can be simply expressed by a function of the type

$$Pa = a - cS + bC \qquad (1.1)$$

where Pa is the wholesale agricultural price level, C total consumption and S the supply of agricultural products.

3 The determination of industrial prices

Since conditions of perfect competition and monopoly in the traditional sense can seldom be found in reality, we can assume that oligopoly — imperfect or homogeneous — prevails in modern industry.

Let us first consider the problem of price determination, and try to postulate it in such a manner as to ease the transition to that of price variation.

We may assume that the firm seeks to maximise its total profits in the long, not the short, period and distinguish three hypotheses, as follows.

I The market for the firm's products is stationary in the sense that, once the equilibrium price has been reached, demand has no tendency to rise or fall; the market for the factors used by the firm is also stationary and factor prices do not change.
II Changes in production methods or in factor prices cause changes in cost, but demand remains constant.
III Product demand varies and tends to increase.

2

Let us begin with the first hypothesis. I have tried elsewhere to work out a theoretical model of price determination[2]; her I shall simply recall its basic assumptions and, hence, the elements determining the equilibrium price.

There are six basic assumptions, as follows.

1   Short-period marginal cost (at given plant) is constant and therefore equal to average direct cost. This assumption seems justified by an increasing number of empirical studies; even though these studies cannot be considered conclusive, the opposite assumption of a U-shaped curve must be discarded, since the arguments brought forward to justify it are open to insuperable objections.[3]

2   The long-period marginal cost curve tends to be L-shaped; with given technology the curve flattens out because of the decreasing effect of economies of scale, whereas diseconomies of scale cannot be conceived as a force gradually pushing up long-period cost. The number of techniques available at a given moment is, however, limited and the long-period cost/quantity relationship should be represented by a limited number of points rather than a curve.

3   When new firms enter the market, those already established go on producing as much as before, not only in order to discourage the entry of new firms but also because otherwise average total cost would rise (it follows from the first assumption that average total cost falls until capacity is fully used).

4   Not all firms have the same power to influence prices. We assume that only big firms can affect prices directly, whereas small firms can influence them indirectly (and involuntarily) by varying their total output.

5   A new firm using a given technique, only enters a certain market if it expects to sell at a price allowing a rate of profit at least a little higher than the market rate of interest; any price lower than that can be considered an 'entry-preventing price'. In the long period the entry-preventing price for a certain type of new firm becomes the 'elimination price' for existing firms of the same category, since they will withdraw from the market if they consistently fail to obtain the minimum rate of profit.

6   An existing firm, using a given technique, is forced to suspend activity or to leave the market if the price falls below the level of direct cost; a price lower than direct cost is an 'elimination price' even in the short period, because the firm cannot go on making losses on its direct cost.

Now, available technologies, factor prices and the position and shape of the demand curve being given, it can be shown that there are various possible equilibrium prices. But only if the initial conditions are neglected

3

is the solution not unique. The final equilibrium price depends on the assumptions made as to the origin of the changes in price or quantity; in practice, it will depend on what firms started the change. In every case, the initial structure of the industry will affect the final equilibrium situation and the variations are irreversible since, *inter alia*, they involve changes in the number of plants. Once these changes have been made there is no going back. Once a certain equilibrium situation has been reached, other equilibrium situations are precluded. In this way 'past history' formally enters into the model. But though there is no unique equilibrium solution in a static sense, something can be said about how prices will be fixed. The equilibrium price tends to settle at a level immediately above the entry-preventing price of the least efficient firms which major firms do not find it expedient to eliminate or absorb by a price war. At the same time, the equilibrium price, given the demand curve for the industry as a whole, will be such as to prevent the entry of new firms, whatever their size.

In short, prices are determined by (1) technologies, (2) factor prices, (3) the absolute size of the market, (4) overall demand elasticity.

The first three of these factors are fundamental. In the case of concentrated (and homogeneous) oligopoly, demand elasticity is relevant only for the industry as a whole and not for the individual firm. In the case of imperfect (or differentiated) oligopoly, demand elasticity seems to have a certain relevance for the individual firm as well. If, however, we assume that in this latter case firms usually differentiate their products not for the sake of higher prices but in order to win the greatest possible number of buyers *at the given price, which is the same for every firm*, demand elasticity becomes irrelevant for the individual firm even in imperfect oligopoly conditions. In other words, apart from the case in which the products are radically different (when it is perhaps more appropriate to speak of so many monopolies rather than of an oligopoly), firms usually consider price differentiation too expensive, because of the probable reactions of rival enterprises, and prefer to differentiate their products rather than their prices. We cannot, in this case, think in terms of individual demand curves.

Therefore, for differentiated oligopoly as well the relevant demand curve is that for the industry as a whole. The equilibrium price is fixed in the way outlined above and cannot be determined from marginal revenue and marginal cost curves.

4

4 *Variations in industrial prices*

We have so far taken the factors determining the equilibrium price as given: techniques and factor prices (which together determine costs), the size of the market and the demand elasticity for the market as a whole.

Let us now suppose (Hypothesis II) that cost varies. We have to distinguish between fixed and direct cost. Direct cost consists of wages, raw material and power costs

$$v = L_i + M_i$$

where L_i is the ratio between hourly wage rates and output per man-hour,

$$L_i = \frac{W_i}{\pi_i}$$

Fixed cost includes salaries as well as depreciation of plant and machinery. Thus we have for total average cost

$$C_T = \frac{W_i}{\pi_i} + M_i + \frac{k'}{x} + \frac{k''}{x} \qquad (1.2)$$

where k' and k'' are the two types of fixed cost and x is the quantity produced.

Only cost changes affecting *all* firms will modify general supply conditions and therefore cause a price change; when cost changes affect a few firms, their supply conditions only will be affected and there is hence no need for a price change.

Changes in supply conditions occur when the prices of variable factors change and when the productivity of labour improves as a result of either new production methods or organisational improvements. Some improvements, however, require large-scale operation and can therefore be exploited only by the larger firms; these firms need not pass on their cost reduction but may instead reap higher profits.

Staff and technicians' salaries are a fraction of total cost, varying from firm to firm; staff composition, moreover, differs very widely. Salary changes will therefore affect all firms but to a much more varied extent than will changes in direct cost. Changes in machine prices will not necessarily influence supply conditions; first, the type of machines used varies widely with the size of firms, and secondly, in a progressive economy machines are written off according to their estimated economic, not physical life, so that there is a big conventional element in depreciation estimates.

Cost changes which alter the equilibrium of the whole market and hence entail price changes are thus essentially of two kinds, both having to do with direct cost: changes in the productivity of labour, for whatever cause as long as they affect all firms, and changes in the price of variable factors. Such changes are frequent even in the short period. Productivity increases almost continuously, though at varying rates, owing both to small technical or organisational improvements and to the effects of important innovations, which may be spread over time; wages and raw material prices, too, change frequently.

Unless business men had quick rules to find the new equilibrium price corresponding to a new level of direct cost, industries would almost always be struggling in chaos; in oligopolistic conditions — unlike in free competition — firms are *not* very small and can directly or indirectly influence prices. One such quick method is full-cost pricing, which is meaningless in a static context but acquires significance when dealing with dynamic conditions and, in particular, when direct cost changes. When such cost changes affect all firms, the price must change, and this change is brought about by a mark-up calculated on the basis of the former equilibrium price. Thus, the new price tends to reproduce the previous equilibrium and to be acceptable to all firms.

In other words, the elements mentioned above fix the equilibrium price; full-cost pricing allows the price to be rapidly adapted to changes in cost, particularly in direct cost.

In its simplest form, the full-cost principle can be expressed as follows:

$$p = v + qv \tag{1.3}$$

where v is direct cost and equals the sum of the cost of labour (w/π) and the cost of raw materials, q is the mark-up, and qv covers the fixed cost per unit at standard volume of output (k/x_n) and gives a certain profit, g, per unit of output. Firms using this formula may be said to apply target mark-up pricing.

If firms charge prices on the basis of a target rate of return (r) on capital invested (K), we have

$$r = \frac{px - vx - k}{K}$$

which implies the following formula, more refined than (1.3):

$$p = v + \frac{k}{x_n} + r\frac{K}{x_n} \tag{1.4}$$

The first formula produces the same result as the second on the assumption that v, k and K vary in the same proportions. The salaries of employees, which represent a sizeable share of fixed cost, k, tend to vary in the same proportion as the wages of production workers. The other share of k — which covers capital consumption allowances — and K (the value of fixed assets) vary in the same direction as the cost of labour and of raw materials, but not necessarily in the same proportion. The simplifying assumption that v, k and K tend to vary in the same proportion is, therefore, not precise, but on the whole seems to be justified. In a first approximation, therefore, in analysing the variations of p one can take the first formula as equivalent to the second. It is worth noting that when the output actually produced and sold, x, is higher (lower) than the standard output x_n, then either the actual profit per unit of output, g (first formula), or the actual rate of profit, r (second formula), becomes higher (lower) than expected.

The hypothesis that price varies as a function of direct cost can be verified using a function of the type

$$Pi = a + b\,\frac{W_i}{\pi_i} + cM_i$$

or, to avoid non-linearity,

$$Pi = a + bW_i - c\pi_i + dM_i \tag{1.5}$$

where M_i stands for prices of raw materials produced outside the industrial sector — in agriculture or abroad. It should be noted that such a relationship is only valid if, at given output per man-hour, marginal cost is assumed to be constant; otherwise it would be impossible to apply the formula to an entire industry and still less to industry as a whole.

Now, if we accept that industrial prices change on the basis of changes in direct cost, must we assume that the mark-up q is constant in every industry?

If direct cost rises, for example because wage increases outrun productivity gains, producers will tend to pass the increase on to consumers; in an open economy, however, they soon run into the obstacle of foreign competition if foreign prices are steady or rising less rapidly. Moreover, in rapidly expanding markets, the bigger firms may find it expedient not to transfer the whole increase in costs onto prices so as not to put a brake on the growth of demand and to avoid the entry of new firms (hypothesis III).

If direct cost falls, for example because productivity gains outpace wage increases, while international prices do not fall, there is no pressure from foreign competition. Either prices will not fall or they will fall only if domestic competition pushes them down in spite of market imperfections and of the power of dominant firms. If *average* productivity rises, as a result not only of generally accessible improvements but also of innovations not open to all firms, prices will necessarily, on average, fall less than direct cost. On the other hand, in rapidly expanding markets the bigger firms may find it expedient to reduce prices in proportion with cost decreases in order to encourage demand and discourage the entry of new firms (hypothesis III).

Two important propositions emerge from this analysis.

First proposition. The mark-up tends to fall when direct cost increases and to increase when direct cost falls. (This is true only for industry as a whole; it may not be true for individual industries and the mark-up may remain constant.)

Second proposition. Short-term price variations depend exclusively on changes in cost, and particularly in direct cost; changes in demand induce corresponding changes in supply without changes in prices. (A sustained increase in demand may affect the extent of price changes; usually — allowing for static and dynamic economies of scale — it tends to check a rise and quicken a decline in prices). This proposition is untrue in only two cases: in the case of an unexpected and large rise in demand — but then the hypothesis of unchanged direct cost is unrealistic; and in the case of a considerable fall in demand — but here, even if the prices of the variable factors remain unchanged, total average cost increases because of the rise in average fixed cost, so that, instead of falling, prices may even increase.

The above proposition is similar to, though not identical with, one of the basic propositions of Keynes's *General Theory*[4]. It seems to hold good, in modern conditions, not only in periods of depression and unemployment, as Keynes believed, but also when the economy expands at a rate that employers consider normal.

I should like finally to point out that the inflationary process cannot be attributed to one cause alone (cost push or demand pull) and that at the same time the eclectic thesis is deceptive; in general it may be said that in industry, except in special cases, the inflationary process is started by a cost push, while for agriculture in the short period — given the supply of agricultural products — it is set off by demand. (This implies, among other things, that a fall in industrial and an increase in agricultural prices, or *vice versa*, may occur simultaneously.) As will be seen, the mechanism governing retail prices is similar to that governing wholesale industrial prices. This difference in the mechanisms in industry and in agriculture gives rise to difficult problems, both theoretically and from the practical standpoint of controlling inflationary tendencies.

5 *Demand, profits and investment*

We must now consider more systematically the third hypothesis, that demand tends to increase. As we have seen, in this case the bigger firms may deliberately choose to raise their price by less than the increase in direct cost, or they may reduce prices by as much as direct cost falls, in order both to discourage the entry of new firms and to favour the expansion of the market and, hence, an increase in production. We have here a first link between price decisions and the growth of the firm's output. But there is another, more important connection. Profits depend on prices (and costs) and investment depends on profits. We must here distinguish between *current* profits and *expected* profits, the former being the source of finance for investment and the latter its motive.

The maximisation of long-term profits is therefore a condition for the maximisation of the rate of increase in the firm's output. It is a necessary but not a sufficient condition, since, to attain its second end, the firm must plough back in investment a part of its profits, while another part must be distributed in the form of dividends (if it is a public company) to support share prices. The amount of external finance (debentures, bank loans) on which the firm can draw also depends on current profits. We can, however, talk of maximisation of the rate of growth only if this rate depends on the firm. This is usually true only within narrow limits. The firm may influence price not only in order to prevent or discourage the entry of new firms (which is here considered to be the overriding concern of oligopolists), but also, as we have seen, to stimulate demand for its products. The firm may also devote part of its profits to advertising campaigns or to diversifying its products in order to raise demand or to speed up its 'spontaneous' increase. The first case is only relevant within certain limits and in certain conditions. The second case concerns only those firms which operate in new fields particularly suitable for expansion. Normally it is difficult to force an expansion of demand and progress mainly depends on the trend of total demand – that is, on exogenous variations deriving not only from the actions of all firms taken as a whole, but also from foreign demand and from the action of the public sector. Here the real problem is no longer one of maximising the rate of development; unless it embarks upon a price war, the firm will attempt to keep pace with the exogenously given rate of increase (possibly with the help of normal advertising), so as to maintain its share of the market.

The relevant connection, therefore, is not so much between profits and output expansion, as between profits and investment. The former directly influence the latter; output expansion, in its turn, is directly influenced not only by investment but also by the trend of total demand.

The long-term maximisation of profits, therefore, in full contradiction with the instantaneous maximisation of marginal analysis, is not to be understood as one single specific target; it implies a complex strategy which, for the purpose of economic analysis, can be studied with reference to three distinct problems, which have been very briefly discussed above: price determination, price change and investment financing.

6 *The investment function for large and small industrial firms*

It follows from assumption 4 (section 3 above) that the larger firms, which can directly influence price because of their considerable market share, regulate production according to variations in demand, while the smaller firms, like those operating in a free, competitive market, produce as much as they can on the one condition that they can make a minimum profit at the current price. The small firms' growth is therefore limited by their own financial means, depending on current profits, and by their possibilities of raising money elsewhere, usually with a bank, again influenced by current profits. Expansion of demand affects the growth and the investment of small firms indirectly, preventing any fall in prices and sometimes allowing the entry of new small firms. The growth of large firms, on the other hand, depends directly on changes in demand, since these firms earn enough to finance a large part of their investment and hence depend only to a relatively limited extent on external finance, especially on bank loans.

Current profits determine the possibilities of financing investment for small and large firms alike. The inducement to invest is given by *expected* profits. Current and expected profits depend not only on the trend of demand but also on the behaviour of prices and costs. We cannot therefore assume, as some economists do, that profits and demand must move together; this is true only when additional assumptions are introduced about prices and cost. Profits as well as demand must therefore be listed among the determinants of investment, and a further distinction should be drawn between current and expected profits; the former affect the source of finance, the latter the incentive to invest.

We can now draw our threads together and write two investment functions, one for large and one for small firms.

The relevant factors for large firms are demand, current and expected profits; for small firms, current and expected profits and the availability of bank loans.

Demand is relevant for the larger firms in so far as it determines the degree of utilisation of their productive capacity. We can therefore consider changes in the ratio between demand and productive capacity, i.e. the 'degree of unused capacity'; this would seem to be the most appropriate expression of that variant of the acceleration principle known as the capital—stock adjustment principle.[5]

Current profits may be expressed by the actual rate of profit (or by the share of profits in income, which moves in the same sense as the rate of profit if the capital/output ratio is constant). Expected profits may be expressed by the rate of change in the rate of profit, or in the share of profits.

Since depreciation funds are normally used to purchase new and better machines which allow of higher labour productivity, it is impossible to distinguish satisfactorily between net and gross investment; we shall therefore use gross investment and, correspondingly, gross profits.

Variations in the availability of bank credit can be measured in terms of variations in the liquidity of the banking system or total liquidity (primary and secondary).

The investment function for large firms may therefore be written

$$I_l = F(UN, G, \dot{G})$$

where UN is the degree of unused capacity, G is the share of current profits and $\dot{G}$ the rate of change of this share.

The investment function for small firms is

$$I_s = f(G, \dot{G}, \dot{L})$$

where $\dot{L}$ expresses the rate of variation in 'total liquidity'.

The aggregate investment function is[6]

$$I = \phi(UN, G, \dot{G}, \dot{L}). \tag{1.6}$$

Before concluding we must ask whether we should consider the *level* or the *rate of change* of investment. It is reasonable to suppose that, if unused capacity is at a low and constant level, large firms will increase their investment; the same will probably happen when the rate of profit is high and constant. From this point of view we should relate the rate of change of investment to the degree of unused capacity and the rate of profit. The answer is not so clear-cut when we consider the other two variables, $\dot{G}$ and $\dot{L}$. Whereas G certainly represents current profits, is $\dot{G}$ an adequate indicator of expected profits? And should we consider the

11

absolute variations (first difference) or the rates of change of total liquidity? The answers to these questions cannot be given *a priori*, and must be based on empirical analysis.

7 The determinants of industrial investment: the degree of unused capacity, the rate of profit, total liquidity

The fundamental determinants of changes in industrial investment are in their turn explained in the model.

We may without hesitation attribute changes in the degree of unused capacity to changes in total demand for industrial products — consumer goods, capital goods and industrial exports. Since in a growing economy a constant degree of unused capacity normally entails an increase in total effective demand (or in its components), we can establish a relationship between the degree of unused capacity and the rates of change in the components of effective demand for industrial products:

$$UN = a - b\dot{C} - c\dot{I} - d\dot{E}_i. \tag{1.7}$$

It is less easy to explain variations in the rate of profit, notably because of the well-known theoretical difficulties involved in the measurement of capital; we can try to avoid them by considering, instead of the rate of profit, the share of gross profits in industrial income — a quantity which businessmen themselves find relevant. Here and later in the empirical analysis we shall almost always use the profit share and not the rate of profit; nevertheless we must at least clarify the links between the two magnitudes, ignoring, for the moment, the difficulties mentioned.

The rate of gross profit, r, equals the ratio between total gross profit, G_t, and capital, K, while the share of gross profits in gross income, G, equals the ration G_t/Y, where Y is gross income. The average capital/output ratio being $u = K/Y$, we have

$$rK = GY$$
$$G = ru.$$

Since we use gross and not net investment, we must similarly use gross and not net profit.[7]

If we assume that the average capital/output ratio is fairly stable in the short period, the profit share and the rate of profit change in the same direction, even if not in the same proportion. This is normally, though not always, true if, over the period, the average capital/output ratio moves in one direction only (either upwards or downwards).[8]

The determinants of the rate of gross industrial profit are industrial prices and variable costs.

Total gross profit, G_t, is made up as follows:

$$G_t = P_i x + L_i x - M_i x.$$

Since $Y = P_i x - M_i x$, the share of profits in gross income may be written

$$G = \frac{G_t}{Y} = \frac{P_i - L_i - M_i}{P_i - M_i}$$

where the cost of industrial labour, L_i, equals the ratio W_i/π_i.

We can use a function of the type

$$G = a + bP_i - cW_i + d\pi_i - eM_i \qquad (1.8)$$

as a linear approximation.

This relation, it is to be noted, is a way of expressing the classical antagonism between profits and wages. Supposing that the mark-up q tends to vary inversely to direct cost (section 4) and that this mark-up, the rate of profit and the share of profits in industrial income all move in the same direction, if follows that the *relative changes of prices and direct cost* (labour and raw materials) *govern variations in income distribution in industry*, which is the leading sector of the economy.[9]

We must now explain the changes in total liquidity. Central banks have come to distinguish three sources of changes in liquidity: the foreign component, government, and the private sector (including state-controlled firms). We can accept this practice and use it in our analysis. Neither the first, which reflects the behaviour of the balance of payments, nor the second, which accounts for variations in the net indebtedness of the state to the banking system, gives rise to any problems. It is less easy to identify a suitable magnitude representing firms' behaviour affecting liquidity. We might take private investment, assuming that the greater it is the more firms have recourse to bank credit, and hence the greater the liquidity created to satisfy this demand for loans. We must however remember that firms turn to banks mainly for short-term credit; typically the demand for short-term credit is raised by increases in overall expenditure on variable factors, notably wages. Wage increases will at a later stage be paid out of increased current receipts, but initially bank loans are needed. We shall therefore use the absolute variations (first differences) of the wages bill to represent the private sector.

These are the three objective factors which govern total liquidity. In our empirical analysis we shall also have to consider the more difficult

13

subjective element, namely, how the central bank reacts to external impulses by using its discretionary powers.

8   *Wages: limits to variations in the rate of increase in money wages*

We have concentrated our attention in this analysis on industrial investment, on the assumption that this is the driving force of the entire economy. Profits are one of the variables which influence investment, and they are in turn influenced by wage changes: if hourly wage rates rise faster than productivity, profits — other things being equal — will fall. As we shall see, wages also influence investment in another way, by affecting the volume of consumption and hence the degree of unused capacity.

We must therefore ask how wages are fixed and how they are changed. We shall again, as with investment, concentrate on industrial wages, and assume that the behaviour of wages in other sectors depends on that of industrial wages. Throughout, industry is considered as the prime mover of the entire system.

In our attempt to explain the determination and — *a fortiori* — the variations of prices, and particularly of industrial prices, we have abandoned the path of traditional marginal analysis. We have assumed constant marginal cost and we have seen that overall demand (for the products of all the firms operating in a certain market) alone has any relevance in oligopolistic conditions; in this case, which is the most frequent in modern industry, price cannot be determined from marginal revenue curves.

Similarly, to explain the behaviour of wages, we have to abandon traditional marginal analysis. [10]

We may consider wages at any moment as determined by the standard of living already attained by the workers — determined, that is, by historical and social circumstances which we must take as exogenous data. [11] We can therefore concentrate our attention on the problem of wage changes.

At a given wage rate, the employer will take on that number of workers that is appropriate to the technique used, which in turn is related to the size of his market share. In a developing economy the entrepreneur plans and builds his plant ahead of demand, so that productive capacity will usually not be full utilised. If demand falls temporarily, capacity utilisation will diminish, working hours will be reduced and some machinery will remain idle. According to our hypothesis, such variations will not influence average variable cost but only average total cost, which will rise because of the increase in average fixed cost. (The temporary fall in demand and production does, however, imply a reduction in average

14

direct cost if all machines are not equally efficient and if it is the less efficient machines which remain idle; but this is a *lower level* of average direct cost and not a *continuous* falling curve of marginal cost.) If, at a given price, the entrepreneur is faced with an unexpectedly rapid increase in demand, he may find it expedient to step up production by using less efficient and hitherto idle machines, by working overtime and by paying higher wages — as long as the higher direct cost still leaves him an adequate margin. His decisions, however, will be made on the basis of averages and not of marginal variations in the true sense.

Employers will constantly seek to introduce improvements so as to increase the average productivity of labour (quantity produced per hour worked). Such increases reduce labour costs (as the ratio between hourly earnings and productivity falls) and raise both unit and total profits. At the same time, when effective demand for their products increases, employers will seek to take on more workers; they will succeed in doing so at the same or only slightly higher wages if unemployment is relatively high, but they will have to pay higher wages if unemployment is low. When wages per hour rise at the same rate as hourly productivity, the relative shares of profits and wages will not change unless raw material or product prices do; when wages increase more rapidly than productivity, the share of profits falls. Assuming a constant capital/output ratio, a fall in the profit share entails a fall in the rate of profit (see section 7 above). If the rate of profit falls below the minimum level, many firms will cut investment and there will be a general recession; unemployment will again rise above the frictional level and the rate of increase in wages will begin to slacken. (The minimum level of the rate of profit may be taken to be close to the long-term rate of interest).

Trade unions exert continuous pressure to raise wages, above all by collective bargaining; during depressions they try to prevent wages falling and, if the cost of living rises, they seek to keep wages in step. When productivity increases rapidly, union claims encounter less resistance from employers, who indeed often increase wages of their own accord in order to keep their labour force and to attract new workers, and then 'wage drift' makes its appearance. [12]

In short, there are two limits to wage variations: an upper limit, given by that rate of increase in wages which, allowing for gains in productivity per hour, will bring the rate of profit down to the minimum acceptable to firms; and a lower limit given by changes in the cost of living. Both limits change over time, because of changes in productivity and in the cost of living.

Since the variation of the upper limit, influenced by changes in hourly

15

productivity, is not the same everywhere, we must expect different rates of change in wages as between different industries and, indeed, as between firms in the same industry when actual total earnings are considered. (It is important to note that the differentials of wage changes and the price movements of individual products tend to iron out inter-industry differences in the rates of profit, but this tendency operates fully only in those industries where barriers to entry are not very high and only in the long period).

All in all, variations in money wages depend basically on three factors: the level of unemployment, changes in the cost of living and changes in productivity per hour. We use the reciprocal of unemployment since, as Phillips has shown, equal percentage changes have different effects at different levels; a 2 per cent change for 10 per cent to 8 per cent, for example, has a weaker effect in pushing up wages than a change from 3·5 per cent to 1·5 per cent. [13] The relation [14] is

$$\dot{W}_i = a + bU^{-1} + c\dot{V} + d\dot{\pi}_i. \tag{1.9}$$

The rates of change in the cost of living, $\dot{V}$, and productivity per hour, $\dot{\pi}_i$, may be considered as the lower and upper limits, respectively, of wage increases; unemployment, U, influences the relative strength of the two opposing groups, workers and employers, and therefore helps to determine at what point in the range fixed by the two limits wages will settle. (Unemployment does not entirely eliminate the area of indeterminacy; unions, like employers' organisations, do not react automatically to objective — favourable or unfavourable — factors, but to a greater or lesser extent use their discretion, which may be affected by legislative or administrative action on the part of government. See Chapter 2, section 7.

The two variables determining the range of money wage increases do not work symmetrically. Let us look at the cost of living first.

There is no doubt that unions plead cost-of-living increases, if any, when renegotiating wage agreements at national or company level. If, as is the case in Italy, wage contracts automatically include an escalator clause it is clear that an increase in the cost of living causes an increase in wages. It is not, however, clear that both will increase in the same proportion. Does a 1 per cent increase in the cost of living lead to a 1 per cent increase in wages? This question can only be answered empirically. In general we can expect that the coefficient of the cost-of-living variable in the equations expressed in rates of change is higher in those countries where an escalator clause is generally applied in wage contracts than in countries where it is not. Where such agreements are standard practice, wage increases obtained at the bargaining table because of increases in the cost of living are over

16

and above those automatically ensured by escalator clauses. This fact, we must point out, need not necessarily have inflationary effects, since, as we shall see, within certain limits a wage rise encourages production without pushing up prices.

Unlike the cost of living, productivity per hour, which is here taken as the upper limit for wage increases, works discontinuously; it puts a brake on wage increases when they become such as to force the rate of profit of a considerable number of firms below the minimum level (approximately the long-term rate of interest). Productivity increases cannot, as an upper limit to wage rises, play the same role as the cost of living does at the lower end of the range; changes in the latter affect all workers in the same way, whereas the former, which influence each firm's ability to pay, are not the same for all firms. It is therefore doubtful whether a clear relationship can be found between the yearly changes in wages and productivity. Such a relationship may perhaps exist when the effective rate of profit of a large number of firms is near the minimum level and wage increases are continually bumping against the upper limit, or when rates of profit do not differ widely.

In any case, this type of problem arises when we seek to explain the trend of *average* wages. From a theoretical point of view the problems of variations in average wages must be kept distinct from those of variations in the wages actually paid by individual industries. Thus there is no doubt that changes in productivity per hour, in so far as they affect the firms' ability to pay, must somehow also affect the wages actually paid by firms wherever trade unions have acquired any power. But this link may not be apparent in *average* variations in wages and productivity, though it might become clear in a disaggregated analysis. Actually it seems that in Italy, in periods of rapid economic expansion, there is a high rank correlation between individual industries ordered according to the rate of increase in hourly earnings and in productivity, which means that the more dynamic industries so far as productivity is concerned, are also the more dynamic from the wages point of view and are presumably those which pushed up *average* wages in the period. We shall return to this point in part II, where we shall also consider other relationships which may help to elucidate some problems of differential wage variations (section 17, below). In the model, for simplicity's sake, we shall concern ourselves only with changes in average wages.

9 *Two determinants of wages: the cost of living and unemployment*

The cost of living is an index made up of the retail prices of commodities, services and rents. Let us begin with the retail prices of commodities.

Conditions of imperfect oligopoly seem to prevail in retail trade. The small shopkeeper is in direct competition with a few others, mainly those in the immediate neighbourhood, and the whole system of retail trade is made up of a chain of such small oligopolistic groups.[15] The boundaries existing between groups, and even within any one group, are the 'imperfections' discussed in the theories of imperfect or oligopolistic competition.

The retailer's main cost elements are the wholesale prices of the commodities he buys and labour costs — the relation, that is, between wages and labour 'efficiency' in retail trade.[16] This 'efficiency' can be expressed by the ratio between the volume of consumer goods sold and the number of workers employed. That is,

$$P_r = a + bP_w + c\,\frac{W_r}{\pi_r} \tag{1.10}$$

where P_r and P_w are, respectively, the retail and wholesale price indices, W_r is the index of wages in retail trade and π_r the index of relative 'efficiency' determined by C/O_r.

If wholesale prices remain stationary but labour efficiency rises less than wages, the cost of labour increases. Italian experience has shown that in retail trade efficiency increases more rapidly in periods of rapid industrial expansion; young workers with some sort of job in trade prefer to move, if they can, into industry, where pay and prospects are generally better, and this tends to reduce overcrowding in trade and to increase efficiency. This happened in Italy during the boom of 1959–1963. In general, however, efficiency has increased less rapidly in retail trade than in industry, and this has contributed to widening the gap between wholesale and retail prices.[17]

The mechanism of retail price changes can be understood only if we remember that foreign competition is totally absent and that domestic competition is less keen than in the wholesale markets of industrial products. It is therefore probable that cost increases are entirely shifted onto the consumer, so that the mark-up remains constant when cost rises. When, on the contrary, cost falls, the mark-up should increase because, owing to market imperfections, the fall in cost is not passed on to the consumer. We can therefore expect asymmetrical variations: the mark-up q will be constant when cost increases and will increase when cost falls. As in the case of industrial prices, the behaviour of q results directly from the sum of coefficients of the rates of change in variable commercial costs.

Concentration enhances efficiency in retail trade, and greater efficiency becomes manifest in smaller retail margins. In other words, where large units — supermarkets, chain stores, etc. — prevail, margins will be narrower than in economies where small units are the rule. The problem of retailing efficiency is, in Italy, particularly serious in the food sector. Though the spread and development of large units can only be a gradual process, public intervention can be effective in reducing inefficiency, particularly, as we have seen, in periods of rapid industrial expansion. Large retail units can exert competitive pressure and reduce the gap between retail and wholesale prices only once they have a sufficiently big share of retail sales, so that competition among them has become relatively strong; otherwise they will not lower prices, but only profit from their lower selling costs.

This point is of great importance, not only from the consumers' point of view but also — what matters much more — from the point of view of growth. An increase in the cost of living due to an increase in retail prices leads to a rise in money wages of no benefit to the worker, whose purchasing power remains unchanged, and of possible harm to the producer, whose labour costs go up. The positive effect which a wage rise might have on growth (an increase in demand) is nullified by the increase in retail prices.

Rent, too, enter into the cost of living. Here again markets are typically imperfect and, as in industry and retail trade, price variations depend mainly on cost variations and not on demand. More precisely, the price of housing depends on building costs and on those of sites. Changes in demand, while not influencing the price of housing directly, do affect the price of building land. The demand for such land depends on the rate of urbanisation; its supply, though influenced by the physical scarcity of land, mainly depends on the speed with which the infrastructures necessary to turn agricultural into building land are created. The price of land has no production costs behind it; it gives rise to rent or, more precisely, to a monopoly gain, since every plot is different from every other. [18]

If we want to explain variations in rents we should therefore resort to a system of two equations. In the first rents (or house prices) vary as a function of the components (wages, productivity, the price of building materials) of production costs proper and of the price of sites; this latter price in turn would be explained as a function of internal migration and of the speed with which infrastructures are created. This model, however, could hardly apply to the whole country; it would have to be worked out separately for individual zones.

In Italy during the period we are considering, legally controlled rents had a preponderant influence in the cost-of-living index used in escalator clauses; rent restrictions, moreover, were gradually eased in the course of the period. Owing to these facts and to the degree of public activity in the field of low-cost housing, rents are considered as an exogenous datum in the model illustrated in part II below.

Lastly, the level of wages is influenced by unemployment, which in turn may be considered a function of investment. Thus, we accept Keynes's propostion that, with a relatively stable propensity to consume, the level of employment will increase only *pari passu* with the increase in investment. [19] This proposition must, of course, be qualified if, unlike Keynes, we assume (1) that the working population is increasing, and (2) that there is technical progress. The first proviso implies that the absolute changes in employment are not equal to those (of opposite sign) in unemployment; the second implies a constant level of employment for a given increase in investment. These qualifications do not prevent the existence of a functional relationship between unemployment and investment, though they affect its shape.

In accordance with the assumption, made throughout, that the important movements of the entire economic system depend on industry, we shall consider industrial investment as the independent variable, while the whole of non-agricultural unemployment will be treated as the dependent variable; in the short period the movement of employed and unemployed workers between industry and other non-agricultural activities is relatively free[20] and we may consider non-agricultural unemployment as a relatively homogeneous aggregate.

10   *The problem of the optimum wage increase*

In the view of employers, the less money wages increase, [21] the better for growth; the optimum would seem to be constant wages and rising productivity. Profits would rise, and profits are both the incentive and the source of investment; the bigger the profits, the greater the investment and the more rapid, therefore, the growth process. We may call this the 'employers' view'.

The trade unions, on the other hand, maintain that the more rapidly wages rise, the more quickly the market expands and the faster, therefore, is the growth process, which also benefits from the faster technical progress induced by strong and continuous pressure from wages. If bottlenecks (monopolistic barriers, inflexibilities of supply) impede progress, it is the government's duty to remove them.

This is a much simplified but, I trust, not misleading picture of the two points of view.

The relative validity of the two opposing points of view – wages as costs or wages as incomes – appears from the preceding analysis. As we have seen, if industrial wages rise more than productivity, raw material prices remaining constant, direct cost will increase *more* than prices. Profits will fall and industrial investment slacken.

On the other hand wage changes, together with changes in the number of wage earners employed, cause changes in the total wages bill. If these workers' propensity to consume is stable and approximating unity, changes in the wages bill induce almost equivalent changes in the demand for consumer goods. This in turn causes a fall in unused capacity and thus stimulates investment. That is:

$$\dot{I} = a - bUN + cG + d\dot{G} + e\dot{L} \qquad (1.6a)$$
$$UN = a - b\dot{C} - c\dot{I} - d\dot{E}_i \qquad (1.7)$$
$$\dot{R} = a + b\dot{W}_i + c\dot{O} \qquad (1.11)$$
$$\dot{C} = a + b\dot{R} \qquad (1.12)$$

$\dot{G}, \dot{L}, \dot{W}_i, UN, \dot{C}, \dot{I}$ and $\dot{E}_i$ we have already encountered, O is employment of dependent labour and R dependent labour income (the dot above the symbol indicates, as usual, the rate of change). All these enter into the model and illustrate the 'trade union view'.

There is, finally, the problem of the balance of payments. Imports of consumer goods and, indirectly, of capital goods vary with changes in wages and in consumer demand. Industrial exports are influenced by income growth abroad and by the behaviour of costs, which determines prices and is itself influenced by wage changes. A wage rise outrunning productivity gains may create a balance-of-payments deficit which in various ways (see section 15 below) can slow down and even temporarily arrest the growth process.

On the other hand, only in the short run will a slower increase in wages than in productivity encourage exports by reducing costs and prices and stimulating producers to seek new outlets abroad. In the long run, as we shall see later, sluggish wage rises encourage neither exports nor growth, because they hinder the expansion of consumption and investment and eventually check the rise of productivity itself. A stagnant or sluggish domestic market does not, moreover, encourage the diversification of production necessary for export growth.

Thus too rapid and too slow wage increases both create problems. In the first case the squeeze on profits and/or balance-of-payments difficulties put a brake on the growth process; in the second case the problems arise from an insufficient expansion of consumption and investment. For the purpose of growth, the optimum rate of wage increases is that

21

which expands demand without squeezing profits and causing a growing deficit in the balance of payments.

At first sight this 'optimum rate' might seem to equal the rate of increase in productivity: if wages and productivity rise at the same rate, labour costs do not increase and profits are not squeezed, while at the same time consumption and investment grow. But this is not necessarily the case.

We must again make a distinction between the short and the long period. While in the short period changes in productivity can be assumed to be independent of changes in wages and employment, this is not so in the long period.

Take the short period first. There are at least three exceptions to the rule that the 'optimum' wage increase is that which coincides with the (given) increase in productivity. First, a faster increase in wages than in productivity need not push up costs and squeeze profits if the price of imported materials is declining. Secondly, when wages and productivity rise at the same rate, the *share* of profits remains constant, but the *rate* of profit will only do so if the capital/output ratio does not change; otherwise, if the rate of profit is to remain the same, wages and productivity must increase at different rates (see section 7 above). Thirdly, if wages should fall behind productivity, the expansion of consumption and investment need not be affected if foreign demand is at the same time growing more rapidly. [22] In the short period, therefore, the optimum rate of wage increase — optimum, that is, from the point of view of growth — does not necessarily coincide with the actual rate of increase in productivity, though it will usually be close to it, except for considerable changes in the countervailing forces.

Productivity gains cannot be assumed to be independent of wage changes and employment in the long period. We must here distinguish between economies with heavy structural unemployment and those without structural unemployment. [23]

Heavy structural unemployment usually entails a low rate of wage increase; static or nearly static unemployment will slow down increases in overall consumption and hence in investment. In the long period a low rate of wage increase may hold back productivity gains, since the pace of mechanisation is influenced by investment expansion and the intensity of wage pressure; [24] technical progress is also checked by the slow growth of income as a whole, of which consumption is the largest part. In such cases public measures to increase wages and raise the propensity to consume of the various income groups will have positive effects on investment and on productivity.

22

If, however, structural unemployment is low and the rate of increase in wages is repeatedly and frequently higher than that of productivity gains, the internal and external difficulties mentioned above will check productivity gains and growth in the long period as well.

The problem of wage increases is, therefore, more complex in the long period. While it is still true that wages and productivity must grow at about the same rate, it should be remembered that the behaviour of the two cannot, in the long period, be considered independent: occasional *temporary* and limited divergences between the two rates may encourage the growth process.

11 *Changes in distributive shares*

Equality of the rates of growth in wages and productivity, at given raw material prices and at a given level of plant utilisation, may seem to imply a constant distribution of income between wages and profits. This is almost exactly true for the industrial sector alone, but when we look at the economy as a whole we must consider, not two, but four distributive shares — wages and salaries, profits (including interest), rents (particularly building rents) and the earnings of the self-employed. To some extent, these last are a pre-capitalist vestige which cannot be broken down to fit into the three traditional categories (wages, profits, rent) of the modern capitalist system; yet rent in a strict sense and self-employed earnings, though scarcely relevant in the industrial sector of a modern economy, may be important in the economy as a whole. Considering the income shares in the economy as a whole, it is clear than an increase in the share of wages and salaries does not necessarily imply a fall in the share of profits, as both might rise at the expense, for example, of the self-employed. [25]

This point is of great importance, since most distribution models consider only the two shares of wages and profits, and conclusions or forecasts as to the trend of overall consumption, as well as of the propensities to consume and to save, are often based on changes in the share of dependent labour income. An increase in this share is not necessarily followed by a fall in the average propensity to save, even if we assume — as we do — that the propensity to save of wage earners is appreciably lower than that of 'capitalists' (out of profits and interest incomes). Thus the fact that in Italy, from 1953 to 1960, the share of dependent labour income and the private savings ratio increased together does not disprove the assumption that wage- and salary-earners have a considerably lower propensity to save than the 'capitalists'; the likely explanation is that the self-employed, whose relative share fell in the period, have a propensity to save about as low as that of dependent workers. [26]

The relevant shares, then, are four, though we have here devoted most of our attention to two of them, wages and profits, because our interest has been concentrated on industry.

The trend of the share of wages in income has been much discussed. Contrary to a once widely held conviction, this share, instead of remaining constant in the long period, appears to have risen considerably, mainly, but not solely, as a result of the progressive fall in the number of self-employed and of a corresponding increase in the number of wage earners. If this is so, it is probable that the share of profits and interest is relatively stable in the long term. Such stability would be the result of the opposing forces described above, which influence the behaviour of wages and profits. Wages cannot grow faster than productivity for long because at some point the system will react negatively, investment will fall, unemployment will rise and the wage increase will be checked. In the opposite case, when productivity increases faster than wages, the growth process, though not coming to an abrupt halt, will slacken owing to an insufficient expansion of demand. But this cannot continue very long because not only the rate of growth but also the rate of increase in productivity will fall; the gap between the wage rise and productivity gains will gradually lessen and the share of profits will cease to grow.

In short, in a capitalist system an increase in the share of wages (unless it is due to shifts from the non-dependent to the dependent labour category), or an increase in the share going to profits and interest, is possible only within certain limits.

12   *Investment and economic relations with the rest of the world*

We have already briefly considered two ways in which foreign economic relations influence industrial investment: through changes in industrial exports which affect the degree of unused capacity, and through the behaviour of the balance of payments which affects total liquidity. We must now consider the behaviour of the main items in the balance of payments. [27]

The most important invisible items in the Italian balance of payments are tourist earnings and capital movements. Earnings from tourism increase more or less steadily; so long as retail prices do not rise much more sharply than in other countries, we may expect this trend to continue, since it depends on the growth of average *per caput* income abroad and on transport facilities. Capital movements, following a distinction made by

24

Marco Fanno, may have a normal or an abnormal character. [28]

Normal movements of long- and short-term capital depend on rates of interest and profit throughout the world. Movements of long-term capital seldom fluctuate greatly from year to year. The central bank has a decisive influence on short-term movements, both via interest rates and by direct intervention *vis-à-vis* the commercial banks.[29] It may therefore be assumed that swings in these capital movements will be particularly large only when the central bank chooses to allow them as means of reinforcing or offsetting total liquidity changes induced by 'objective' factors. Hence, large short-term capital movements may be considered as one of the means adopted by the central bank for purposes of restrictive or expansionist policy; in other words, this is a possible manifestation of that discretionary element introduced into the model by means of the 'dummy variable' in the equation for liquidity.

Abnormal capital movements are often associated with political factors, such as the periodic waves of mistrust unleashed by fiscal or economic measures viewed with disfavour by capitalists. The most important abnormal capital movements nowadays, however, seem to be those set off by expectations of devaluation following a serious balance-of-payments crisis, and therefore they depend on the previous behaviour of the balance of payments. Since the other invisible items either move according to a fairly well-defined trend or are relatively stable, the balance of payments tends to move with the trade balance (even if the sign is not necessarily the same). We may therefore concentrate our attention on changes in the trade balance, at least for a country like Italy. [30]

Imports vary with changes in income and in the ratio of domestic to world prices. More precisely, imports of consumer goods (IM_c) and investment goods (IM_I) depend on consumption and investment demand, respectively. Visible exports vary directly with changes in world demand and inversely with the ratio of domestic to world prices.

$$IM_c = a + bC + c \frac{P_c}{P_{woc}} \tag{1.13}$$

$$IM_I = a + bI + c \frac{P_I}{P_{woI}} \tag{1.14}$$

$$E = a + bWD - c \frac{P_E}{P_{wo}} \tag{1.15}$$

where P_c and P_I are domestic prices of consumer and investment goods, P_{woc} and P_{woI} are world prices for the same two categories of goods, WD is world demand and P_E are export prices.

If domestic price changes are moderate and close to those prevailing elsewhere, we may expect that domestic income (or world demand) will be the major factor in determining changes in imports (or exports). It should also be remembered, in considering the ratio of domestic to world prices, that the export price of a product may differ from the price at which the same good is sold at home. Even in the absence of customs duties various factors can be responsible for such a difference: transport costs, for instance, or marketing advantages which the domestic producer enjoys in his own country thanks to his knowledge of local usage and law, his possibilities of making long-term contracts with retailers, or his control of the distribution system. As a result, export prices rise less than domestic prices, or do not rise at all, in inflation periods.

Exports are also influenced by the trend of domestic demand. If it is rising rapidly and if prices are rising, producers will find it expedient to dispose of their increasing output on the easier and more profitable home market. Exports, therefore, depend on world demand and on the ratio of domestic to world prices, and also on domestic demand.

II Empirical aspects

13 *Preliminary questions: reliability of the data, economic significance of the aggregates*

The reliability of the data used is very important. The mere fact that empirical verification does not confirm a theoretical hypothesis need not mean that the hypothesis is invalid; responsibility may lie with the terms of its formulation, the suitability of the series used, or, what concerns us here, the reliability of the statistics.

We have here adopted two criteria in judging the reliability of the data. First, the reliability of economic statistics is influenced both by the manner of their compilation and by the facts underlying them. Employment and unemployment figures, particularly those regarding agriculture, and the average prices of agricultural products are among the most unreliable. Secondly, variations are always more reliable than absolute levels.

The question of statistical reliability partly overlaps with that of the logical meaning of aggregates and averages. The problem of aggregation should be considered case by case; in some cases aggregation is possible or meaningful only if the behaviour of the basic series is of one type and not another. For example, aggregation of direct costs at the level of an individual industry or for the industrial sector as a whole is logically possible only if we assume that total cost is a linear function of output (that is, if marginal cost is constant). Apart from these cases, aggregation influences the values of the parameters and of the constant in the equations and makes their interpretation problematic; however, if the relationships considered have real economic meaning, they are neither disguised nor obscured by aggregation.

14   *The model for the Italian economy*

The assumptions behind the equations used and, in some cases, the specific form that they should take, were outlined in part I. Here we shall merely reproduce the model (Table 1.1) and comment on the equations fitted, particularly on those which for some reason differ from what theoretical analysis would have led us to expect.

This model is only a first attempt to combine theoretical and empirical analysis into one organic whole, and the author, who is not an econometrician, is aware that it has various limitations.[31] But work of this kind is rare, particularly in Italy; if the attempt is fruitful, others who are better equipped can make more comprehensive and sophisticated studies and, by comparison with other industrial countries, can establish what results are generally valid for all of them.

The equations have been estimated on the basis of statistical series for the period 1951–1965; each equation has been separately fitted by the least squares method.

For each coefficient we give its *t* (how many times the value of the coefficient is greater than the standard error) and the significance of the coefficient itself (per cent probability that the value obtained is not a random value).

In some equations the variables are absolute values, or index numbers expressing absolute values, in others they are rates of change or first differences. The theoretical reasons for the choice of one or the other form have been explained in part I. Generally speaking we avoided absolute values when the variables to be explained and all (or some) of the independent variables show an obvious trend; in these cases the risk of multicollinearity is high and is best avoided by using rates of change or first differences.[32] Both equations in absolute values and equations in rates of change are therefore used in the model; hence the need for a number of identities to transform absolute levels into rates of change and *vice versa*.

Some of the equations used are similar to or identical with equations already used by others (those for industrial prices and wages, for example); others imply almost intuitive links and hardly need comment; yet others are here proposed for the first time (agricultural prices, retail prices of goods, industrial investment, total liquidity).

Some subsidiary equations have also been fitted in order to verify a particular hypothesis or to eliminate or reduce uncertainties in the equations of the model itself (Table 1.2). Comments follow the order and numbering of the equations used in the model; 'subsidiary' equations have the same number as the corresponding equations in the model, plus a letter.

1   The equation for *agricultural prices* has already been discussed (section 2 above). Demand is given by the total flow of private consumption at current prices; available supply is the algebraic sum of home production and net imports, all quantities measured at constant prices.

It might seem improper to consider net imports in addition to home production, since the former partly depend on demand for consumption goods, which is the other explanatory variable. However, we are considering an *ex post* relation; thus, when domestic demand for agricultural products increases more than production, prices can remain constant only if an increase in imports causes total supply to rise in proportion to demand. But such an increase may not occur, for various reasons (customs barriers and import restrictions, transport costs, world-wide scarcities, and others). The price rise in agricultural markets is a precise measure of the tension resulting from disequilibrium between demand and supply, however caused. From this standpoint it seems justified to consider total supply, and not only domestic production. In any case, a variant of the equation for agricultural prices using home production instead of total supply has been calculated; the result is almost equally good: for the first equation R^2 is 0·927, for the second it is 0·917 (equations 1 and 1a).

The equations in the model are based on the series of the new National Accounts. Two other equations for agricultural products as a whole have also been fitted, using the data of the National Institute of Agrarian Economics *(Istituto Nazionale di Economia Agraria)*; in the first the flow of consumable goods is expressed at current prices (as in the equation used in the model), in the second at constant prices. These equations, too, give very good statistical results, both for R^2 and for the relatively small standard error of the coefficients (equations 1b and 1c).

Lastly, equations have been estimated for particular classes of products (fruit and vegetables, and meat and dairy products)[33]; both likewise give statistically good results (equations 1d and 1e).

SYMBOLS

Endogenous variables

P_a = farm prices (here considered as equal to wholesale agricultural prices)

P_i = wholesale industrial prices

P_w = wholesale prices

G = index of the share of profits (manufacturing industry)

P_r = retail prices

V = cost of living

W_i = hourly earnings in manufacturing industry

C = personal consumption (v = at current prices, c = at constant prices)

R = dependent labour income

I = industrial investment (at constant prices)

U = percentage of non-agricultural unemployment

UN = percentage of unused capacity (manufacturing industry)

L = total liquidity (ΔL: first differences at end-year)

IM = total imports at current prices

E = total exports at current prices

E_i = industrial exports at current prices

TB = trade balance

Exogenous variables

S = supply of agricultural products (home production + net imports)

π_i = index of hourly productivity in industry

π_r = index of productivity in retail trade

A = index of rents

T = net indebtedness of the Treasury

B = dummy variable, liquidity equation (1961 and 1962: +1; 1951 and 1964: −1; other years: 0)

WD = world demand

M_i = index of raw material prices

Other symbols: R^2 = coefficient of determination; ˙ = rate of variation; Δ = first difference; τ = time index.

Table 1.1

The model – Equations fitted

(with the econometric collaboration of Dr Elio Ugonotto)*

			R^2	t (coefficients)	Significance (%)	DW†
1 Agricultural prices	P_a	$= 122\cdot400 - 0\cdot774\,S + 0\cdot772\,C_v$	0·927	6·69 3·35	99 99	1·57
2 Industrial prices	P_i	$= 48\cdot738 + 0\cdot249\,W_i - 0\cdot223\,\pi_i + 0\cdot492\,M_i$	0·908	5·91 4·94 3·55	99 99 99	1·35
3 Industrial investment	I	$= -64\cdot381 + 0\cdot761\,G - 2\cdot553\,UN + 0\cdot832\,\dot{L}$	0·989	5·59 7·34 1·97	99 99 95	1·82
4 Unused capacity	UN	$= 13\cdot353 - 0\cdot521\,\dot{C}_c - 0\cdot158\,I - 0\cdot113\,E_i$	0·811	1·81 3·23 2·73	95 99 99	1·74
5 Industrial profits	G	$= -3\cdot703 + 1\cdot155\,P_i - 0\cdot793\,W_i + 0\cdot706\,\pi_i$	0·927	3·83 7·68 6·80	99 99 99	1·82
6 Total liquidity	ΔL	$= 899\cdot835 + 2\cdot096\,TB - 1\cdot064\,\Delta T + 1\cdot520\,\Delta R$ $+ 702\cdot815\,B$	0·978	11·39 3·23 19·89 8·35	99 99 99 99	1·43
7 Industrial wages	$\dot{W}_i$	$= -0\cdot621 + 18\cdot903\,U^{-1} + 1\cdot198\,\dot{V}$	0·855	6·61 18·19	99 99	2·09
8 Wages in retail trade	W_r	$= 37\cdot427 + 0\cdot572\,W_i$	0·988	22·71	99	—
9 Retail prices	P_r	$= 30\cdot134 - 0\cdot122\,\pi_r + 0\cdot455\,P_w + 0\cdot375\,W_r$	0·987	1·43 4·24 8·14	90 99 99	1·89
10 Non-agricultural unemployment	U^{-1}	$= 0\cdot083 + 0\cdot041\,I$	0·910	11·51	99	—
11 Dependent labour income	ΔR	$= -26\cdot003 + 129\cdot170\,\dot{W}_i$	0·787	6·65	99	—
12 Private consumption	ΔC_v	$= 0\cdot845 + 0\cdot005\,\Delta R$	0·904	10·70	99	—
13 Imports	IM	$= -19\cdot878 + 0\cdot760\,C_v + 0\cdot396\,I$	0·979	9·67 4·16	99 99	1·28
14 Exports	E	$= -67\cdot013 + 1\cdot679\,WD$	0·983	26·97	99	—
15 Industrial exports	E_i	$= -3\cdot076 + 1\cdot027\,E$	0·998	219·50	99	—

Identities and definitional equations

1 Wholesale prices	P_w	$= 0 \cdot 204\, P_a + 0 \cdot 796\, P_i$
2 Industrial investment	I	$= \Delta I + I_{\tau-1}$
3 Industrial wages	W_i	$= \Delta W_i + W_{i\tau-1}$
4 Cost of living	V	$= 0 \cdot 934\, P_r + 0 \cdot 061\, A$
5 Cost of living	V	$= \Delta V + V_{\tau-1}$
6 Private consumption at current prices	C_v	$= \Delta C_v + C_{v\tau-1}$
7 Private consumption at constant prices	$\Delta C_C/\Delta C_{c\tau-1}$	$= 0 \cdot 906\, \Delta C_v/C_{v\tau-1}$ $- 0 \cdot 724\, \Delta V/V_{\tau-1}$
8 Trade balance	TB	$= 31 \cdot 08\, E - 42 \cdot 08\, IM$

* Dr Ugonotto gave fundamental econometric help in the estimation of the parameters and, in part, in the specification of the relationships; he supervised the preparation of the programmes, organised the statistical data and helped in their collection, choice and analysis; he instructed those who joined the project at a later stage; helped to free the reduced form of the model of the inevitable formal imperfections resulting from its long gestation and to complete the links necessary for its correct functioning; his collaboration lasted for the fifteen months of the statistical verification and was financed by the CNR.

Dr Ugonotto will present, and comment on, the reduced form of the model in a forthcoming article. The results seem positive; for example, the model 'foresees' the recessions of 1958 and 1964 satisfactorily.

† The Durbin—Watson test does not indicate the presence of positive or negative autocorrelation in any case; in five instances however (equations 2, 4, 6, 9 and 13) the test is indeterminate for a positive autocorrelation: it neither suggests nor excludes it.

Table 1.2

Subsidiary equations

			R^2	t (coefficients)	Significance (%)
1a Agricultural prices	P_a	$= -119.918 - 0.017\,S_h + 0.751\,C_v$	0.917	5.99, 2.93	99, 99
1b Agricultural prices	P_a	$= 108.512 - 0.503\,S + 0.514\,C_v$	0.892	3.13, 6.08	99, 99
1c Agricultural prices	P_a	$= 117.223 - 0.378\,S + 0.284\,C_c$	0.909	2.96, 6.77	99, 99
1d Fruit and vegetable prices	P_f	$= 68.256 - 0.377\,S_f + 0.761\,C_v$	0.862	2.06, 5.30	95, 99
1e Meat and dairy prices	P_m	$= 112.553 - 0.360\,S_m + 0.223\,C_v$	0.822	3.26, 6.01	99, 99
2a Prices of industrial goods	P_i	$= 0.084 + 0.400\,L_i + 0.386\,M_i$	0.758	3.85, 4.25	99, 99
2b Furniture prices	P_{fu}	$= 2.274 + 0.186\,\dot{W}_{fu} - 0.516\,\pi_{fu} + 0.635\,M_{fu}$	0.953	1.80, 4.72, 7.70	90, 99, 99
2c Textile prices	P_t	$= 1.564 + 0.332\,\dot{W}_t - 0.325\,\pi_{tu} + 0.364\,M_t$	0.703	3.17, 2.54, 2.24	99, 95, 95
3a Industrial investment	I	$= 39.188 - 1.932\,UN + 0.840\,G - 1.099\,i$	0.867	4.07, 4.21, 0.73	99, 99, 75
6a Total liquidity	ΔL	$= 818.139 + 1.195\,TB + 1.140\,\Delta T + 1.518\,\Delta R$	0.828	3.94, 1.29, 6.29	99, 90, 99
7a Industrial wages	$\dot{W}_i$	$= 5.567 - 0.463\,U + 1.386\,\dot{V}$	0.837	2.53, 5.20	99, 99
7b Industrial wages	$\dot{W}_i$	$= 2.020 - 0.396\,U + 1.488\,\dot{V} + 0.381\,\dot{\pi}_i$	0.883	2.38, 6.15, 1.99	95, 99, 95
7c Industrial wages	$\dot{W}_i$	$= 4.830 + 15.878\,U^{-1} + 1.201\,\dot{V} + 0.403\,r_{\tau-1}$	0.887	2.01, 4.37, 1.36	95, 99, 90
9a Retail prices	P_r	$= 1.483 + 0.740\,\dot{P}_w + 0.211\,L_r$	0.722	1.97, 4.99	95, 99
9b Retail prices	P_r	$= 0.067 + 0.620\,\dot{P}_w + 0.359\,\dot{W}_r$	0.793	3.00, 4.64	99, 99
10a Non-agricultural unemployment	U	$= 17.055 - 0.158\,I$	0.866	9.17	99
11a Dependent labour income	$\dot{R}$	$= 1.530 + 0.861\,\dot{W}_i + 1.360\,\dot{O}_n$	0.753	5.72, 3.24	99, 99
11b Dependent labour income	ΔR	$= -239.559 + 67.545\,\Delta W_i + 1.258\,\Delta O_n$	0.842	7.48, 2.85	99, 99
13a Total imports	IM	$= -0.507 + 21.831\,X + 1.083\,\dot{C}_v + 0.409\,I$	0.861	5.32, 2.37, 2.88	99, 95, 99
14a Exports	$\dot{E}$	$= -0.381 + 1.415\,WD$	0.666	4.90	99
15a Industrial exports	$\dot{E}_i$	$= 36.884 + 1.025\,WD_i - 0.399\,P_{iE}/P_{iwo}$	0.620	2.75, 2.10	99, 95

1a $\dot{S}_h$ = domestic agricultural production.

2a $\dot{L}_i$ = rate of change of the cost of labour: W_i/π_i.

3a i = long-term rate of interest.

6a Does not include the dummy variable B.

7c r_{T-1} = rate of profit (de Meo), lagged by one year.

9a $\dot{L}_r$ = rate of change of labour costs in retailing: W_r/π_r.

11a and 11b $\dot{O}_n$ and $\Delta \dot{O}_n$ = rate of change and first difference of non-agricultural employment.

13a X = dummy variable: 1957–58: −1 (abnormal fall in the value of imports, due to the fall in raw material prices following the US recession); 1959–60: +1 (exceptional rise in imports, probably influenced by the start of the Common Market).

15a $W\dot{D}_i$ = world demand for industrial products, rate of change; P_{iE}/P_{iwo} : ratio between export prices and world prices of industrial products.

2   Direct costs are used as the independent variables in the equation for *industrial prices*. For the sake of linearity, labour cost has been taken as the difference, and not the ratio, between wages per hour and productivity per hour. The index of prices of imported raw materials has been adopted on the assumption that technical progress in their use is negligible, at least in the short period. [34]

The conclusion reached in section 4 that the mark-up should increase when direct cost falls and diminish when the latter increases, has been tested by fitting an equation of the type

$$\dot{P}_i = \gamma \dot{L}_i + \gamma \dot{M}_i$$

where $L_i = W_i/\pi_i$ and the dots over the symbols stand for rates of change; [35] clearly the mark-up q is constant if $\delta + \delta = 1$, whereas it will vary inversely to direct cost $(L_i + M_i)$ if $\delta + \delta < 1$.

The results confirm the hypothesis: the correlation is good and the sum of the coefficients of the two components of variable cost, equal to $0\cdot79$, is less than unity by a non-negligible amount (equation 2a). The result applies to manufacturing industry as a whole. To eliminate the possibility that it is an optical illusion due to aggregation rather than the outcome of a genuine economic relation, it would be desirable to test it at the individual industry level – no easy task, because of the difficulty of collecting homogeneous series of data. To obtain some rough indication, however, we calculated the parameters relating to a few individual industries. The results are similar to those for the aggregate equations: the sum of the coefficients of wages and raw materials is $0\cdot82$ for textiles and $0\cdot69$ for furniture (equations 2b and 2c).

3   The equation for *industrial investment* is substantially as expected. Investment and total liquidity are expressed as rates of change, while the degree of unused capacity and the share of profits in gross industrial income are expressed in percentage terms. (The share of profits and not the rate of profit has been used for the reasons discussed in part I). The coefficient of the rate of change in the share of profits, which was considered as an index of expected profit, is not significant. The hypothesis cannot, however, be discarded out of hand; non-significance may be due to the data used and not to the absence of a genuine economic relationship. Nor is the long-term rate of interest (equation 3a) significant as an explanatory variable; here, however, there seem to be valid theoretical reasons for rejecting changes in the interest rate as a major influence on investment.

As for total liquidity, the rate of change rather than first differences appears to be significant.

4   The equation for the *degree of unused capacity* corresponds exactly to what was expected. The fact that the coefficients of the three independent variables (private consumption, investment and industrial exports) also correspond fairly well to their weights lends credibility to the result. All three variables are expressed in rates of change (see section 7 above).

5   Strictly speaking, the relation for the *share of profits* in gross industrial income is not an equation but an identity.[36] In the model, however, it appears as an equation ($G = a + bP_i - cW_i + d\pi_i$), for two reasons: (i) some of the data on which the share of profits has been calculated are not homogeneous with respect to those for prices and for the elements of direct cost; (ii) this identity would have implied a non-linear relation between some of the terms which also appear in other equations, whereas we are interested in a linear relation. In the calculated equation, the coefficient for imported raw materials is not significant and has therefore been omitted. Non-significance in this case may be due to the data used or to the fact that the index of imported raw material prices varied only slightly in the period.[37]

6   *Total liquidity* depends on the state of the balance of payments, on changes in net Treasury indebtedness towards the banks and the public, and on changes in the total wages and salary bill. As has been seen, the trade balance may be used in place of the whole balance of payments. Since we are concerned here with the *flow* of total liquidity, we considered the first differences for total liquidity itself, for Treasury indebtedness and for the wages bill; for the trade balance, we used its absolute value at current prices.

However, changes in liquidity cannot be held to depend exclusively and automatically on these 'objective' factors. The central bank's decisions, although influenced by such factors, can enhance or mitigate their effects to a greater or lesser extent. This discretionary element has been included in the analysis by means of a 'dummy variable' to which the values of -1, 0 and $+1$ have been given. The variable has been assigned the value of $+1$ in those years in which the central bank unequivocally and deliberately followed an expansionist policy (strengthening any 'spontaneous' expansion), the value of -1 in years of deliberate credit restriction, and a zero value in year of 'neutral' policy, when the discretionary element was unimportant because the central bank probably created liquidity as the 'objective' factors indicated, without trying to influence their effects on liquidity. The use of annual data requires that we consider banking policy prevailing over each year as a whole, or at least over the greater part of the year.

35

The values assigned to variables are bound to be somewhat arbitrary and those other than zero have therefore been used sparingly, only for those years when there were many and unequivocal reasons for doing so. [38]

The dummy variable noticeably improves the fit: R^2, which is 0·828 without the dummy variable (equation 6a), rises to 0·978 when the dummy variable is introduced and all the coefficients, including that of the dummy variable, have a 99 per cent significance. Technically speaking, the central bank can carry out its expansionist or restrictive policies in various ways; the method most commonly used in recent years is that of granting, refusing or limiting the commercial banks' faculty to borrow abroad.

The dummy variable in some sense expresses the specific discretionary behaviour of the monetary authority or, for those who prefer it, of the governor of the central bank.

7 and 8   There are two equations for *wages*, one for industrial wages and one for those in retail trade, the latter being 'explained' by the former in accordance with our assumption that industry is the mainspring of the economy.

The use of absolute levels may be justified despite the risks of multicollinearity (wages show a sharply rising trend) for the second equation, which is subsidiary to the first, but the first equation cannot be treated in the same way and is therefore written in terms of rates of change.

Several versions of this equation were fitted, using the cost of living, non-agricultural unemployment and hourly productivity, or industrial profits, among the variables; rates of change have been adopted for the cost of living and hourly productivity, which show obvious trends, while unemployment and profits are expressed in percentages. The cost of living (whose changes are taken as the minimum limit of wage variations) and the percentage of non-agricultural unemployment are always significant, as is the rate of change in hourly productivity (equation 7b), although barely so. The doubts expressed for theoretical reasons in section 8, and arising mainly from the large inter-industry dispersion of the rates of change in productivity (and profits) which makes the use of averages of very doubtful validity, are not dispelled by empirical analysis. [39] We therefore used in the model an equation including only unemployment and the cost of living as independent variables.

For reasons already explained overall non-agricultural and not merely industrial unemployment has been adopted, and the reciprocal of that type of unemployment is used. [40] (R^2 is 0·855 when we use the reciprocal of unemployment, which is in principle preferable, and only slightly lower – 0·837 – when we use instead the simple unemployment percentage (equations 7 and 7a).

The coefficient for the cost of living (rate of change) is greater than unity in both the linear (1·39) and non-linear (1·20) variants. Here interpretation is not easy; since we are trying to explain changes in total earnings, and since the escalator clauses apply only to contractual wages (usually about 60 to 70 per cent of total earnings), the coefficient for the cost of living should be about 0·6 or 0·7. On the other hand, in part I we considered changes in the cost of living as the floor of wage changes; this hypothesis might appear confirmed by a coefficient greater than unity, the 'excess' being due to trade union pressure which, *ceteris paribus*, increases with the cost of living. The picture, however, remains cloudy; the coefficient of the rate of change in the cost of living does not in fact need to be equal to or greater than unity in order to support the 'minimum limit' interpretation, which only implies that the actual increase in wages must be at least equal to the rise in the cost of living, whatever brings about this result. In conclusion, no specific economic meaning must be attached to the precise value of this coefficient, which depends on the simultaneous action of the factors considered.

Furthermore, as we shall see later, the above coefficient may very well be equal to or greater than unity without foreshadowing an explosive wage–price spiral.

As in the case of liquidity, a discretionary element – pertinent to the trade unions and/or the government – enters into the determination of wages (section 8 above). No such element was included in the model, for the sole reason that we were unable to devise a practicable way of setting the values of a dummy variable. [41] However, the presence of this discretionary element should not be neglected, though probably its action is usually of little importance. Formally, it may be held responsible for the greater part of the 'unexplained' variances in the wage equation; in particular, in 1962 the estimated value is about four points lower than the actual value, probably as a consequence of the demonstration effect of the very considerable increase in civil service pay awarded by the government. In 1965 and 1966, on the other hand, the estimated values are higher, by 1·4 and 2·0 points respectively, than the actual values. The deliberately moderate policies followed by the trade unions were perhaps due to their appreciation, after the 1964 experience, of the negative effects on investment and employment of an excessive increase in wages.

9   The equation for *retail prices* is similar in structure to that for indus-

trial prices, with the important difference that the mark-up should be about constant and hence the sum of coefficients relating to the components of direct cost, in the variant considering rates of change, should be approximately unity. This hypothesis, too, is confirmed (equations 9a and 9b). As has been seen (section 9 above), however, the mark-up q should remain unchanged only when direct cost increases, whereas it should rise − the sum of these coefficients, that is, should be appreciably greater than unity − when direct cost falls. This hypothesis could not be tested because direct cost fell in only one year (1959) of the period. We also tried to detect the influence of changes in indirect taxation on retail prices, but the result was negative, probably because such an influence cannot be seen in a disaggregated analysis (section 9 above).

10   The percentage of *non-agricultural unemployment* has been related to the absolute level of investment, as would seem to follow from one of Keynes's propositions (section 9 above). The results are good from a statistical point of view even when we use the percentage of unemployment; they are yet better when we use its reciprocal (R^2 rises from 0·866 to 0·910 − equations 10a and 10). The reason for non-linearity seems to be clear; a given increase in investment has effects of decreasing intensity on unemployment, as investment rises and unemployment falls. (Owing to technical progress and to the increase in the labour force, the function relating investment and the unemployment reciprocal is likely to change over time; however, this complication can be neglected in considering relatively short periods like ours).

11 and 12   In the first of these two equations the dependent variable is *dependent labour income* and the independent variables are industrial wages and non-agricultural unemployment. In the second, dependent labour income is the independent variable and the dependent variable is the *flow of private consumption* (at current prices). First differences are used because the variables in both equations are on a rising trend.

These two equations pose no particular problems of interpretation. The criterion of omitting inessential variables was followed once more; thus, in the equation for dependent labour income (equation 11), industrial wages are the only independent variable, in line with our assumption that other incomes follow those in industry, and dependent employment is not considered so as not to encumber the model unnecessarily (R^2 is about the same when dependent employment is included − see equations 11a and 11b). Again for the sake of simplicity, dependent labour income is the only independent variable for private consumption, on the following assumptions: that wage earners' propensity to consume is close to unity, that the self-employed have a similarly high propensity to consume and that their income moves together with dependent labour income, while the consumption of other social groups is of relatively secondary importance.

13, 14 and 15 Lengthy comment on the equations for *economic relations with the rest of the world* is unnecessary. Imports are explained largely by changes in private consumption and in industrial investment, and exports by changes in world demand. The influence of the ratio of domestic to world prices is not significant. The price effect may actually be of minor importance; it may also be that its action is concealed by the high degree of aggregation in the model. The latter possibility finds some support in the fact that, in the equation 'explaining' the rate of change in *industrial* exports, the price coefficient is significant and has the right sign (equation 15a). In the equation for exports the attempt to test the influence of domestic demand (a fall in home demand should increase the incentive to export) failed, either because of aggregation or, more probably, because of the fact that domestic demand only declined absolutely during a part of 1964.

Industrial exports (whose rate of change is one of the variables explaining the degree of unused capacity) are simply explained by total exports.

The two equations for imports and exports in the model are expressed in absolute terms. Since imports, exports and their respective independent variables are all on a rising trend, this is an exception to the practice here adopted of using rates of change when the dependent variables and at least one of the independent variables show a trend over time. The exception is due to the fact that the trade balance is arrived at by subtraction of absolute values for imports and exports; the use of rates of change for these two flows was technically possible but would have required other identities (to obtain the absolute levels) and burdened the model excessively. [42] Subsidiary equations for imports and exports were calculated using rates of change; the results are good from a statistical point of view, though not as good as those obtained from the equations with absolute levels.

15 *Implications of the model: limits to the wage—price and consumption—investment spirals*

Though a model is a set of equations in which all variables are interdependent, some fundamental sequences can be identified; interdependence is not incompatible with cause and effect. More precisely, the variations caused by a change in any one of the elements can be seen throughout the system and those which seem most significant can be closely observed. Here we shall only consider wage—price and consumption—investment sequences, both of which have been much discussed from various points of view. Several writers suggest that the problem of explosiveness inherent in both could be solved by determining the range of values of the relevant parameters compatible with stability, but without enquiring into the economic meaning of the maximum values. As we shall try to show here, the problem of 'explosion' arises from an oversimplification of the relations considered.

Let us first examine the limits to a rising wage—price spiral.

Wages can increase for reasons which are endogenous or exogenous to the model. An immediate endogenous reason would be a fall in unemployment. Exogenous factors which influence wages via the cost of living are, for example, a bad harvest or restrictions on agricultural imports, or an increase in rents.

Let us assume that industrial productivity is increasing at a 'normal' rate and that some exogenous factor causes industrial wages to start rising considerably faster than productivity. Equation 2 tells us that wholesale industrial prices will rise. Wholesale agricultural prices may also tend upwards because the increase in wages affects demand. If employment remains constant or increases, dependent labour income will rise (in the latter case by more than wages); private consumption will increase and wholesale agricultural prices will rise if the consumption of agricultural products grows more than available supply (equation 1). The increase in both industrial and agricultural prices raises the cost of living (assuming that the other components, retail margins and rents, do not fall) and this rebounds on wages, pushing them up even further. The increase in consumption for its part stimulates investment (equations 3 and 4), increased investment reduces unemployment and pushes wages, and hence prices, even higher.

While these mutually reacting impulses tend to bring about a self-generating and even 'explosive' spiral, there are offsetting factors which sooner or later may stop and reverse the trend.

Equations 2 and 5 tell us that, when industrial wages grow at an appreciably higher rate than productivity, the share of industrial profits falls; hence industrial investment is depressed (equation 3),[43] unemployment rises (equation 10) and consequently the rate of increase in wages slows down (equation 7).

The faster increase in consumption and investment, moreover, by speeding up import growth (equations 11, 12, 13), causes a deterioration in the trade balance and hence a squeeze in liquidity creation (equation 6); as a consequence investment falls and unemployment rises.

A deterioration in the trade balance is usually accompanied by a worsening of the balance of payments (section 12 above). If the deficit is considerable the central bank may decide to squeeze liquidity creation further (the dummy variable B in equation 6 becomes negative); again investment will fall and unemployment increase.

Of course, wages may cease to rise at a rate which forces prices up if one of the exogenous factors triggering off the acceleration ceases to operate or even goes into reverse — if, for example, the supply of agricultural products begins to rise enough to satisfy demand or if rents stop going up.

Thus, the preceding analysis shows clearly that important forces in the model itself prevent an explosion of the wage—price spiral. The requirement that the coefficients in the wage and price equations should not exceed certain values — e.g. that the coefficient of the cost of living should be below unity — only arises when an insufficient number of equations is considered, that is, when the action of the countervailing forces is neglected. [44]

The preceding analysis also shows up the one-sidedness of the view which sees credit restriction and a contrived increase in unemployment as the remedy for inflation. There are many more counters in the game, and the public authority can act directly on some of the factors (agricultural imports, rents, retailing efficiency) [45] that influence the cost of living. It does, however, remain true that in certain cases, particularly when the balance-of-payments deficit is increasing rapidly, intervention must be immediate and wide-ranging in its effect and that it is difficult to avoid credit restrictions unless measures regarding other factors have been prepared in time. On the other hand, as was pointed out in section 8, trade unions can decide whether to exploit a favourable situation to the full or to keep their wage claims within moderate limits. In the former case the long-term effect may be harmful to the unions and to the workers as a whole, mainly because of the resulting increase in unemployment.

In any event, the forces influencing wages and prices are certainly more complex than many diagnoses and proposed cures would suggest.

Much the same may be said about the interaction between consumption and investment, which is the essence of the multiplier—accelerator models of business cycles or growth. Here, too, it has been maintained that the accelerator and multiplier must not exceed a certain range of values if explosion is to be prevented, but in a less simple analysis the problem of explosion does not arise. Our model, though relatively simple, perhaps avoids artificial explanations of spurious problems because it contains an analysis not only of certain major aggregates but also of certain important categories of wages and prices.

Let us assume that an external impulse affects investment; it might be an increase in foreign demand for industrial products, or expansionist policy on the part of the central bank. An increase in industrial exports or in liquidity causes an increase in investment (equations 4, 6, 3), a fall in unemployment (equation 10) and, hence, an increase in wages and consumption (7, 11, 12) (the working of the multiplier may be seen in this way). The rise in consumption in its turn reduces the degree of unused capacity and therefore drives up investment (4, 3) (this is the acceleration principle or, more precisely, the capital—stock adjustment principle). The spiral would continue upwards if it were not first braked, then stopped and reversed, by counter-impulses similar to those already considered: rising wages due to falling unemployment will at a certain point squeeze profits and hence damp down investment. [46] The increase in investment and consumption, moreover, has an adverse effect on the trade balance and this checks the creation of liquidity; if the deterioration is serious, liquidity creation may be further and drastically checked by an independent decision of the central bank.

A last general observation. The model mainly refers to the modern sector of the Italian economy, and it might seem that the archaic or pre-capitalistic sector — which is very extensive, expecially in the South — has been excluded. In fact, its presence is felt in the model in various ways, mainly indirect or exogenous: through retail trade (more or less backward everywhere in Italy), through agricultural production, [47] and through non-agricultural unemployment, whose level depends, among other things, on the flight from the land.

It must, however, be made clear that the role of the pre-capitalistic sector in the model is essentially passive.

16 The turning points of 1958 and 1963—64

The turning points of 1958 and 1963—64, which had very different origins, may be clarified by this type of analysis.

The 1958 downswing originated abroad. World demand levelled off as a result of the US recession, and Italian exports, particularly of industrial products, barely increased during the year. [48] The consequences of such a slow-down are clearly visible in the model: the fall in the rate of export growth increases unused capacity, industrial investment is checked and the slow-down thus spreads.

The recession which began in the last quarter of 1963 and lasted until the beginning of 1965 was largely internal and much more complex in origin. This recession was preceded by a quick rise in wages, consumption and investment. The wage rise was basically due to the rapid diminution of unemployment and to the increase in the cost of living. [49] The share of industrial profits began to fall as far back as 1960–61 (see graphs in the Appendix): from 1961 on, wages rose increasingly faster than productivity and were perhaps decisively responsible for this decline. The *rate of increase* in investment fell with the profit share, but investment continued to rise, though at a dwindling rate, because the increase in private consumption was still affected by the rising wages bill and by the liberal policy of the central bank (its policy, in 1962 and in the first half of 1963, was too liberal, which, as is now clear, was a mistake). Three contrasting forces thus affected investment: one negative – the fall in profits – and the other two positive – the increase in consumption, which kept the level of unused capacity low, and the exceptionally rapid expansion of liquidity, which directly stimulated investment. In 1963 and, more clearly, in 1964 the negative force prevailed and investment fell in absolute terms; unemployment therefore rose and the rate of wage increase was checked; this in turn caused consumption to fall, unused capacity to rise and investment to fall further. [50]

At the same time the rapid increase in the wages bill and in consumption and the rise, though at a decreasing rate, of investment caused a mounting deficit in the trade balance and, eventually, in the balance of payments; total liquidity therefore fell, with a depressing effect on investment. The recession became acute and widespread as a result of the credit squeeze by which the central bank attempted to correct the balance-of-payments deficit. This recession was one of the most serious and persistent of postwar years; it would have been graver if the favourable international economic situation had not allowed a relatively high rate of export growth.

17 *Useful relationships for further development of the analysis*

The model has been kept relatively simple, at the cost of no little effort, in order to bring out certain fundamental theoretical points. For any further development of the analysis certain exogenous variables would have to become endogenous to the model and others would have to be disaggregated. Industrial productivity, for instance, should be treated as an endogenous variable. The well-known 'Verdoorn's law', recently discussed by Kaldor, suggests the existence of a direct relationship between output and productivity. Although convincing and important,[51] this relationship has been omitted from the model so as to avoid additional variables — industrial production in this case — and also because the 'law' is much less clear for relationships between annual series than for the cross-section of different countries or industries analysed by Verdoorn and Kaldor.

The link between growth of output and growth of productivity is shown by the rank correlation coefficients for different industries; an inter-industry analysis of this type avoids the uncertainties arising from aggregation. Presumably, also, productivity increases are greater in larger undertakings (large size allows both static and dynamic economies of scale). Lastly, a disaggregated analysis may bring out the influence of productivity on wages which was obscure when considering changes in *average* wages and in average productivity (section 8 above).

The Spearman rank correlation coefficients have been calculated for certain groups of phenomena. The results seem encouraging, even if they reveal the need for a more detailed and yet more disaggregated analysis.[52]

		Value of the rank correlation coefficient
1.	Output per man-hour and production, 1953–64	0·90
2.	Output per man-hour and degree of concentration[53]	0·76
3–4.	Earnings and output per man-hour:[54]	
	1951–61 (period of rapid expansion)	0·68
	1961–64 (less rapid expansion and recession)	0·38
5.	Earnings (1953–61) and degree of concentration	0·78
6.	Earnings, output per man-hour and degree of concentration	0·72

The influence of foreign competition in restraining prices when cost rises (section 4 above) was tested by calculating the correlation coefficient between the pressure of foreign competition and price changes in a period of rising costs and prices in fourteen industries.[55] The results are fairly good, if not excellent: the correlation coefficient is $-0·83$ and R^2 is $-0·689$.

Lastly, as a curiosity and as an appendix to the equations for profits and liquidity, we calculated the coefficient of multiple correlation between industrial share prices, the profit share, total liquidity and share prices in the United States (the leading capitalist economy): R^2 is good (0·814) and the coefficients are all significant, though at different levels. [56]

18   Parameters, variables and structural changes. A mental experiment

As in all models, not only the values of the parameters but the variables of the equations themselves are historically conditioned. The relationships which the equations seek to describe work within a certain structural and institutional context; when it changes, the parameters and the relevant variables must also change.

We can illustrate this point by a mental experiment, to use Schumpeter's phrase. What variables, were the data or estimates available, would have been relevant in the past, say a hundred years ago?

Let us look at the equations for wholesale agricultural and industrial prices, retail prices, investment and wages in industry.

The agricultural price equation would scarcely be different. Agricultural markets were competitive in the past and are competitive now — with the exception, today, of those for certain major products where a minimum support price is in effect. Though the parameters would certainly differ, there is no reason to suppose that the relevant variables would do so.

Concentration has profoundly changed the structure of modern industry. In the past there was competition among numerous small enterprises in several industrial sectors, which were also more important. Today oligopoly prevails. The equation for industrial prices in the past would therefore be different from the one used in this study, and presumably more similar to that for agricultural prices.

The equation for retail prices, on the other hand, would probably not undergo any important change, not even in the value of the parameters. This especially applies to a country like Italy, where modernisation of the sector has only just begun.

The equation for industrial investment, by contrast, would be very different. When industrial markets were much closer to the atomistic competition of classical theory, investment probably varied as a simple function of profits, as classical theory teaches. [57] Perhaps also the extent to which firms were able to get bank credit influenced investment (given the existence of imperfections in the loan market). Neither the degree of unused capacity nor any other indicator of the pressure of demand was probably very important; in competitive conditions firms have no interest

45

in producing less than their full potential output, except in crisis periods. Changes in unused capacity become important when growing concentration in industry increases the influence of demand in investment and production decisions.

The rate of change in the cost of living would probably not have appeared among the relevant variables in the equation for wages — which, like all the equations in the model, refers to the short period. This is not only because escalator clauses are of recent origin but also, and much more so, because trade unions either did not exist or were much weaker a century or half a century ago than they are today; as has been said, the unions exploit changes in the cost of living, independently of escalator clauses, in their wage bargaining. [58] Moreover, changes in productivity nowadays influence wages directly since union pressure for wage increases is stronger when employers' net margins are known to be increasing. The rate of change in productivity would therefore not appear among the variables relevant a century ago, and the wage equation would be much simpler, with the rate of change in wages in the short period depending on unemployment alone, as Marx maintained. While we can only make guesses for the other equations, the studies of Phillips and Lipsey on the interpretation of wage movements in England provide some empirical verification. These studies cover a very long period — almost a century — and seem to demonstrate convincingly that changes in retail prices became important as one of the explanatory variables of wage changes only in the last five or six decades, and especially after the first world war. Before that date wage changes could in large part be 'explained' by the percentage of unemployment (more precisely by its reciprocal). The two authors, and especially the former, have unwittingly offered an empirical test of a proposition first put forward by Marx, showing at the same time that, expressed in those terms, it applies only to a certain historical period.

Our mental experiment would need to be supplemented by comparative empirical verification, that is, by applying the equations of the model to the data of other industrial countries. Since the model refers to the modern sector of the Italian economy, it is likely — though not certain — that the relevant variables will turn out to be the same, economic structures being similar, whereas the parameters, which reflect the conditions peculiar to different economies, cannot but be different, perhaps considerably so.

Postscript (1973): Historical change and econometric models

The model illustrated in the preceding pages was worked out in 1966 and 1967 with the help of Dr Elio Ugonotto and was first published at the end of 1967. Subsequently, Dr Carlo Del Monte extended the model to the period 1951–1970 and also worked out its simultaneous solution. In so doing, he found it necessary to introduce a number of changes which raise some fundamental questions regarding the correct formulation and use of econometric models.

Generally speaking, when the period covered by an econometric model is extended, it may prove necessary to make one or several of the changes listed below in increasing order of importance:

(a) some, possibly slight, adjustment in the coefficients of certain equations, leaving the equations themselves structurally unaltered;

(b) some equations may have to be altered substantially, with the addition of new explanatory variables;

(c) some equations may need revision in order to improve their interpretative value;

(d) one or more new equations may have to be introduced for the sake of a satisfactory simultaneous solution;

(e) the model as such may prove unsatisfactory, so that an entirely new one has to be constructed (this will obviously happen after a profound social upheaval, after a war, say, or a revolution).

Faced with this list of possibly required changes, the model-builder has to ask himself why they are necessary. There are three possible reasons: (1) the original data may have been imperfect; (2) one or more of the equations may have been theoretically erroneous or not satisfactorily specified, which the model-builder may realise on second thoughts or when new analytical tools come to hand; (3) the economy under observation may itself have changed. Changes under (2) and possibly those under (1) are subjective in the sense that they have to do with the observer or observers; those under (3) are objective and belong to the category of historical change.

In bringing our model up to date, changes of the kind (a), (b) and (c) appeared necessary. Only those under (c) owe anything to 'progress' on the part of the observer, in so far as the equations concerned might have been presented in their new version already in the original model, regardless of its subsequent updating. Those under (a) and (b), on the other hand, are most probably, at least in part, attributable to historical changes.

Table 1.3

Updated and revised model (C. Del Monte)*

			R^2	t (coefficients)	DW
1	Agricultural prices	$\dot{P}_a = 109.66 - 0.257\,S + 0.0025\,C_v$	0.95	9.49 1.85 6.36	0.66
2	Industrial prices	$\dot{P}_i = -0.167 + 0.297\,\dot{L}_i + 0.316\,M_i + 0.459\,\dot{P}_{iwo}$	0.84	0.47 4.10 2.82 3.99	1.95
3	Industrial investment	$\dot{I} = -51.99 - 2\,UN + 0.501\,\dot{L} + 0.898\,G + 18.34\,DI$	0.96	6.08 12.99 1.46 8.67	2.42
4	Unused capacity	$UN = 15.412 - 0.577\,\dot{R} - 0.128\,\dot{I} - 0.192\,\dot{E}_i + 0.016\,I_{\tau-2}$	0.93	14.58 9.23 4.84 5.03 2.95	1.56
5	Industrial profits (share)	$\dot{G} = -1.355 - 0.967\,\dot{L}_i + 0.670\,\dot{P}_i$	0.64	2.11 5.40 2.28	1.96
6	Total liquidity	$\Delta L = 886.398 + 1.729\,TB + 0.586\,Z + 1.434\,\Delta R + 830.286\,B$	0.98	5.90 6.70 2.39 14.64 5.87	1.25
7	Industrial wages	$\dot{W}_i = -0.760 + 0.720\,\dot{V} + 17.680\,U^{-1} + 6.58\,DW$	0.93	0.54 5.02 3.40 4.95	1.23
8	Wages in retail trade	$W_r = 39.594 + 0.685\,Wi_{\tau-1} + 61.034\,U^{-1}$	0.99	18.25 43.04 4.37	1.18
9	Retail prices	$\dot{P}_r = 0.668 + 0.453\,\dot{W}_r + 0.560\,\dot{P}_w$	0.80	4.63 5.33	2.89
10	Non-agricultural employment	$U^{-1} = -0.085 + 0.00051\,I + 0.00094\,I_{\tau-1}$	0.93	4.67 2.42 4.22	0.96
11	Dependent labour income	$\Delta\dot{R} = 78.48 + 41.55\,\dot{W}_i + 3352.85\,U^{-1}$	0.93	0.46 6.90 2.98	1.57
12	Private consumption (current prices)	$\dot{C}_v = 2.429 + 0.608\,\dot{R}$	0.64	1.94 5.48	1.59
12a	Private consumption (constant pr.)	$\dot{C}_c = 0.854 + 0.776\,\dot{C}_v - 0.642\,\dot{V}$	0.87	1.68 10.19 5.95	1.05
13	Imports	$IM = -18.061 + 0.662\,I + 0.0265\,C_v + 28.674\,DIM$	0.90	3.11 4.90 8.27 2.98	2.01

Identities and definitional equations

Wholesale prices	$\dot{P}_w = 0.169\,\dot{P}_a + 0.791\,\dot{P}_i$
Cost of living	$\dot{V} = 0.958\,\dot{P}_r + 0.091\,\dot{A}$
Trade balance	$TB = 10.27\,E - 12.01\,IM$
Agricultural prices	$\Delta P_a = P_a - Pa_{\tau-1}$
Industrial profits (share)	$G = \Delta G + G_{\tau-1}$
Industrial wages	$W_i = \Delta W_i + Wi_{\tau-1}$
Total liquidity	$L = \Delta L + L_{\tau-1}$
Dependent labour income	$R = \Delta R + R_{\tau-1}$
Industrial investment	$I = \Delta I + I_{\tau-1}$
Imports	$IM = \Delta IM - IM_{\tau-1}$
Private consumption (current prices)	$C_v = C_v + Cv_{\tau-1}$
Wages in retail trade	$\Delta W_r = W_r - W_{r\tau-1}$

NEW SYMBOLS

P_{iwo} = International prices of finished industrial products

Z = public debt

DW = dummy variable, wage equation

DI = dummy variable, investment equation

DIM = dummy variable, imports equation

*Reproduced from Carlo Del Monte, 'Un modello econometrico per l'economia italiana utilizzato a fini previsivi', Rassegna economica 1, 1973.

The most important subjective change concerns the new equation for unused capacity, where lagged investment (two years) was introduced to allow for capacity increases due to prior investment. This change was proposed by Dr Del Monte. On the objective side, the most important changes are in the wage and investment equations.

A few comments have already been made (section 18 above) on changes in the wage equation attributable to historical changes on the labour market. In extremely simplified terms it can be said that a century ago and indeed up to the first world war, short-period wage variations could be explained with the help of only one explanatory variable, namely unemployment. Thereafter, with the growing strength of trade unions, the cost of living, too, became relevant. But even this is not enough for the most recent years, when the discretionary power of trade unions became so great that it now has to be accounted for by a third variable which somehow expresses, directly and in quantitative terms, the unions' militancy. Accordingly, an index based on the number of man-hours lost through strikes was introduced into the wage equation to account for 'trade union pressure', which certainly has increased very much in recent years not only in Italy, but in many other industrial countries – a new, historical fact. For the sake of simplicity, a dummy variable (DW) was used in the revised model; I did the same on another occasion with US data and got good results. (The rationale of the new wage equation is explained in Chapter 2, section 7.)

Likewise, a new dummy variable was introduced into the equation for industrial investment during the period 1966–70; in this case the chief purpose of the dummy is to account for the acceleration of investment (especially of the labour-saving type) attributable, with a lag, to the wage explosion of 1962–64 (see also Chapter 4, section 8) and for the faster pace of public-enterprise investment after 1967, for investment by firms in the public sector is governed by factors which only in part coincide with those affecting investment by private firms strictly speaking. Again, it was only for the sake of simplicity that a dummy was used in the revised model; the rate of increase in public-enterprise investment would have done just as well.

The revised model, then, takes account of a number of historical changes. Any attempt to do so, of course, rests on a particular view of economic analysis and its methodological implications. This view is that the subject matter of economic analysis changes in time not only quantitatively, but qualitatively and irreversibly; it is this which gives it its historical character. It is a view that ultimately can be traced back to two of the greatest economists, Adam Smith and Karl Marx.

In stressing the historical aspect of the subject matter of economics, I do not in any way wish to belittle the value of economic theory or, for that matter, of econometric models. History and theory are not incompatible. But theoretical and, more especially, econometric models do have their limitations. These are serious enough when models are used for analysing and interpreting what has happened, but almost crippling when it comes to forecasting. After all, some major 'new fact' may emerge during the very period covered by the forecast.

Strictly speaking, the word forecasting should not be used at all. It would be better to say conditional predictions, or simulations, or hypothetical projections. The explicit assumptions refer to various values — regarded as reasonable or plausible, but always up to a point arbitrary — assigned to the exogenous variables; but there is an underlying implicit assumption as well, and this is that during the period covered by the simulation the economic system will not change — or at any rate, since this is impossible, that it will not change in any important respect. However, when it comes to formulating assumptions about the exogenous variables or some working hypothesis about isolated structural changes, the model-builder has to do some research and collect well-founded information from experts or from leading protagonists in various fields, like the public sector, the money market, and the labour market. Some of the exogenous variables may be decisional variables, in so far as as their value depends on the decisions of, say, the government, the central bank or trade unions. There is all the more reason, in these cases, to search out all available information; this kind of research is not part of model construction, but must precede it. There is all the more reason, too, for not attributing predictive value to simulations of the future. The future is not written in the stars; it depends on what human beings will do. Models merely serve to render explicit the dynamic interdependence of objective factors and of the leading decision centres.

In any event, the results of simulation must always be confronted critically with the information at hand. Agreement or compatibility enhances confidence in the results of simulation; in the contrary case the analysis has to be carried further, in an attempt to identify the source of the most valid indications. It is only by such a dialectic process, as it were, that we can hope to achieve real progress in critical knowledge and make a serious attempt to form a critical opinion on the likely course of events in the near future.

Notes

[1] This, in substance, is also Ricardo's view.

[2] *Oligopoly and Technical Progress*, Harvard University Press, revised edition, 1969; 'Prices and wages: a theoretical and statistical interpretation of Italian experience' *Journal of Industrial Economics* no. 1, 1967.

[3] There are two main arguments. The first, based on the principle of diminishing returns, supposes that plant and machinery must be used as an indivisible whole. The second is based on considerations of demand: unusually high demand causes cost to rise for one or more of the following reasons: (1) workers are paid overtime rates; (2) less efficient machines are brought into use; (3) additional and usually less efficient labour has to be paid at the existing wage rate.

Now, the hypothesis of plant and machinery having to be used as an indivisible whole very seldom corresponds to reality; the concept of the 'degree of unused capacity' implies the use of some or all of numerous similar machines or of machines whose output varies according to their running time. The hypotheses behind the second argument may justify two − or three − levels of marginal cost, but not a gradually and continuously rising curve; unusually high levels of demand, moreover, cannot help to identify an equilibrium position. The third hypothesis is only valid if equal wages are paid to unequally efficient workers. It should be noted that Keynes thought this factor of pre-eminent importance in causing cost to rise after a certain point (*General Theory*, pp. 41 and 299), though he considered rising cost as usual, but not necessary. For a discussion of the whole question see also P. Garegnani, 'Note su consumi, investimenti e domanda effettiva' *Economia Internazionale* no. 4, 1964, and no. 5, 1965, note 1, p. 72 of the reprint.

[4] The proposition − which assumes constant techniques − according to which supply is very elastic up to the point of full employment and inelastic thereafter. An increase in effective demand therefore causes production and employment to increase at almost constant prices until full employment is reached, whereupon it is reflected, entirely or predominantly, in higher prices. Keynes, op. cit., pp. 295, 300, 304−5.

[5] The acceleration principle is usually expressed by the function

$$I = f(\dot{Y})$$

where I is investment and $\dot{Y}$ the rate of change in income. The capital−stock adjustment principle is expressed by a function of the type

$$I = F(Y, K)$$

or often, in linear form, by a function of the type

$$I = aY - bK$$

in which lags are introduced.

The connection between this formula and that using the degree of capacity utilisation is clear from the following relationship:

$$U_g = Y_e/Y_{max}$$

where U_g is the degree of utilisation, Y_e actual production and Y_{max} maximum potential output. If we consider the ratio between the capital stock and maximum potential output, $u^* = K/Y_{max}$, then

$$Y_{max} = K/u^*$$

and therefore

$$U_g = \frac{Y_e}{K} u^*.$$

⁶ The relevant causal relation is therefore from profits (as well as demand and liquidity) to investment, and not *vice versa*. 'Animal spirits' may explain something, but they scarcely help to explain short-term investment changes. See my *Oligopoly and Technical Progress*, op. cit., pp. 188–96.

⁷ The above relationship can be modified to consider 'net' profits by including depreciation as a percentage of capital. The formula becomes $G_n = ru + k/K$.

⁸ The above conclusion is normal but not necessary, since, for example, r may increase if u falls more rapidly than G. In the short period, however, changes in u are small and exceptions to the 'normal' case are rare.

⁹ This model, unlike recent neo-Keynesian theory, allots no part to the average and marginal propensities to consume of the various social groups in determining the distribution of income or changes in it.

¹⁰ Constant short-period marginal cost (plant given) does not necessarily imply that the marginal productivity of each variable factor is also constant. Mathematically speaking, marginal cost is a simple, and marginal productivity a partial, derivative. The economic significance of a partial derivative in our case would seem to be irrelevant: an additional weaver, for example, cannot weave the air, he must be given the amount of cotton or wool required by the techniques used. Marshall was aware of this and always spoke of the *net*, not *marginal*, product of labour; by net product he meant the increase in the value of the product 'after deducting for any

extra expenses', i.e. the additional expenses incurred for raw materials and other things in employing an additional worker (*Principles of Economics*, eighth edition, 1949, pp. 337 and 427–31).

The notion of a partial derivative is clear-cut and Marshall (rightly) did not imply it, since he was considering the increase in production due to a *simultaneous* increase of the variable factors – quite a different thing.

The average productivity of variable factors, understood as the inverse of the input of each variable factor (production coefficient or the quantity of a factor used per unit of product) is perfectly admissible and it is true to say that, at given techniques and constant marginal cost, average productivity is constant. If, as it does, average productivity varies over time, this is not due to changes in the quantity produced but to changes in technology. Gardner Ackley, in a simple but convincing inquiry, supports the view that average productivity is generally constant for variations in productivity. He continues, however, to make the customary assumption of 'diminishing returns' on grounds similar to those given by Hicks for continuing to assume generalised competition. (G. Ackley, *Macroeconomic Theory,* Macmillan, New York 1961, pp. 95–101; J. R. Hicks, *Value and Capital*, Oxford 1946, p. 84).

The above refers to the short period, when plant is given. The possibility of using marginal productivity, in a rigorous sense, in the long period may exist but becomes irrelevant if we pose, as I do, the problem of the choice of techniques in discrete, not continuous terms.

[11] This approach has some connections with that of the classical economists and was suggested by Pierangelo Garegnani.

[12] In the empirical analysis presented in part II, actual earnings per hour have been adopted and the problem of the relationship between them and constractual wages has been neglected. In my view, wage drift is essentially due to competition among employers to hold workers or to attract labour and is largely independent of the absolute level of contractual wages (which is mainly due to trade union pressure). Competition among employers in the labour market may for example raise actual earnings 10 per cent over the contractual level; this 10 per cent increase would occur, in my opinion, whether the contractual level were 100 or 90 or 110; it is due to rivalry among employers in a relatively tight labour market.

[13] The full titles of Phillips's study and of other empirical studies quoted in the text are given in the Appendix.

[14] Various economists have proposed equations of this type; some stress unemployment (Phillips and others), others, like Kaldor, profits, and yet others (Lipsey, Perry) occupy an intermediate position. The difference

between their work and the present study lies not so much in the variables considered as in the analysis of the links between the independent variables and the rate of change in wages.

[15] See T. N. Wolfe (who quotes Kaldor), 'The Problem of Oligopoly' *Review of Economic Studies* no. 56, 1953–54, p. 181.

[16] Strictly, the 'cost of labour' can only refer to shopkeepers employing paid assistants; for the others the 'cost of labour' is at most a hypothetical term, not necessarily valid in the short period. It should be added that retail prices are probably also influenced by indirect taxation. Such an influence, however, is likely to show up only in a disaggregated analysis.

[17] In Italy, wholesale prices remained, on average, stationary between 1953 and 1961, retail prices rose by about 1·5 per cent a year and the cost of living (which also includes services and rents) by about 2·5 per cent.

[18] Cf. A. Breglia, *Reddito sociale*, Ateneo, Rome 1965. A simple but effective measure of the behaviour of building 'rent' is given by the ratio between the index of average rents for a certain town and the index of building costs; when the ratio is constant, building 'rent' is unchanged, an increase means that the price of sites, and hence building 'rent', is rising.

[19] *General Theory*, op. cit., pp. 98 and 113.

[20] Obstacles to the movement of workers from agriculture to other activities are considerable; only the building industry absorbs agricultural workers at all readily.

[21] The assumption of falling money wages appears unrealistic in present conditions and is not considered.

[22] This happened in several years between 1953 and 1960. Wages between 1961 and 1963, on the other hand, rose 'excessively', with adverse effects on the economic situation in 1964. This was only the second instance – the other was 1906–7 – of an 'excessive' wage rise in the century which has elapsed since the unification of Italy; the trouble usually was the opposite – wages usually rose *too slowly*. (The example of 1906–7 was pointed out by G. Fuà.)

[23] L. Meldolesi suggested this distinction, which also forms one of the premises of Garegnani's, Note su consumi, investimenti e domanda effettiva', op. cit.

[24] See R. Rostas, *Comparative Productivity in British and American Industry*, Cambridge University Press, 1948.

[25] This probably happened in Italy between 1951 and 1960; the share of wages and that of industrial profits both increased, while the share of self-employed income fell, mainly because the number of self-employed declined. The share of both wages and profits would have increased more if the share of building rents had not also risen.

[26] The common opinion that the savings propensity of the self-employed is appreciably higher than that of dependent workers is based on the behaviour of heads of households and not on that of independent workers as a whole; the savings propensity of the numerous family workers in the category is probably very near unity, though the question needs much more statistical study.

[27] This section draws on ideas put forward by Franco Modigliani in a seminar at the Bank of Italy in April 1965, and on a largely empirical study by Sergio Sgarbi, who fitted the 'foreign' equations in the model.

[28] M. Fanno, *Normal and Abnormal International Capital Transfers*, University of Minnesota, Minneapolis 1939.

[29] F. Masera, 'International Movements of Bank Funds and Monetary Policy in Italy' *Banca nazionale del lavoro Quarterly Review*, December 1966.

[30] For our purposes (since the trade balance is one of the determinants of liquidity) what matters is the *direction* of changes in the trade balance, not its level or its sign; the trade balance and the balance of payments are assumed to move together, and the inclusion of the trade balance alone simplifies the model.

[31] For example, unlike in the real world, almost all the relationships in the model are linear, hence they are only valid for moderate changes in the various quantities.

[32] To simplify the model, absolute levels have been used in three cases where rates of change or first differences would have been indicated; as a check, subsidiary equations using rates of change were also fitted in all three cases.

[33] Other classes of products could not be considered because the available price and output series were defective. Fruit and vegetables and meat and dairy products are, however, among the most important groups in Italy at the present stage of economic development.

[34] Strictly speaking, a suitably weighted average of domestic agricultural products and of imported raw materials should have been used, since both are *external* to the industrial sector as a whole; for simplicity, we used the index of imported raw material prices, which includes some agricultural commodities.

[35] The non-linear form presents no difficulties here; it verifies a hypothesis and does not enter the model.

[36] The behaviour of the share of profits and the rate of profit (calculated by De Meo, see Appendix, item 4 in the bibliography) is generally similar, though with variations in the amplitude of fluctuations. 1961 is an exception: a relatively strong dip in the capital/output ratio caused the

share of profits to fall while the rate of profit continued to rise (see section 7 above).

[37] The share of profits in gross industrial income — the variable to be explained — has been calculated with the formula $\dfrac{VA - W_b}{VA}$ or $\dfrac{G_t}{VA}$, where VA is value added, W_b the wage and salary bill and G_t total gross profits. Since value added is obtained by subtracing from total receipts $(P_i x)$ the total expense for raw materials $(M_i x)$, and the wage and salary bill can be seen as the product of the expense for workers and employees per unit of output $(L_i = W_i/\pi_i)$ and total output (x), we have

$$\frac{G_t}{VA} = \frac{P_i x - M_i x - L_i x}{P_i x - M_i x} = \frac{P_i - M_i - L_i}{P_i - M_i} .$$

This ratio precisely expresses the share of profits in gross industrial income.

[38] The value of $+1$ has been assigned for 1961 and 1962, and -1 for 1951 and 1964. Though the credit restrictions began in September 1963, the year 1963 as a whole has been awarded a zero since expansionary policies continued into its early months. See P. Baffi, A. Occhiuto, M. Sarcinelli, 'Per la storia della politica monetaria in Italia' in *Letture di politica monetaria e finanziaria*, Banca Popolare di Milano, 1965; P. Baffi, *Studi sulla moneta*, Giuffrè, Milan 1965.

[39] The wage equation has been tested with various profit indices (the share of profits, the rate of profit in the same year, the rate of profit in the preceding year) as well as with productivity per hour. The rate of profit in the preceding year (equation 7c) alone approached significance. The lag might be due to the unions obtaining notable (or modest) wage rises in year τ if the end-year profits of year $\tau - 1$ are notable (or modest). This argument is rather artificial and the coefficient is in any case on the borders of significance. In a similar equation for the United States, also for the postwar period, profits are clearly significant (G. L. Perry, pp. 50–51). Calculations made, like Perry's, on a quarterly (or monthly) basis with a three-month lag may be better suited to the purpose, particularly because moving averages can be used, and this may have influenced Perry's results. There may, however, be a real difference in the behaviour of profits in the two countries, for example because profits in America may, on average, have moved closer to minimum levels. As has been suggested in the text, the use of averages for this type of relation may not be justified (at least in economies where differences in profits and in profit variations are as wide as in Italy).

[40] Since, as we shall see, the reciprocal of unemployment is also used in the equation explaining unemployment, no problems arise in the model due to non-linearity.

[41] This was written in 1967. Subsequently I think I have found a device for quantifying this discretionary element. See Chapter 2, section 17.

[42] The trade balance is the only link with the foreign component; since imports and exports (and the related explanatory variables) are expressed in index numbers (1963 = 100), whereas the absolute value of the trade balance is required, they have been multiplied by the coefficients 42·98 and 31·08, respectively (the value of imports was 4,298 billion and that of exports 3,108 billion lire in 1963).

[43] A fall in profits will cause a fall in investment when the counter-vailing forces are insufficient; the former essentially depends on the fact that when direct cost rises, domestic and foreign competition prevents prices from rising to the same extent (equations 2 and 2a) (section 4 above) and profits are squeezed. A fall in profits causes, or may cause, a fall in investment, but not *vice versa*.

[44] The problem is encountered in single-equation and two-equation models, where one relates to prices *in general* and the other to wages; see e.g. Lipsey (Appendix, item 6 in the bibliography).

[45] For instance, the increase in agricultural prices, partly due to import restrictions (particularly on meat and dairy products) and bad harvests, had a considerable influence on the exceptionally rapid rise of wages in 1962 and 1963.

[46] The 'full employment ceiling' (see J. R. Hicks, *A Contribution to the Theory of the Trade Cycle*, Oxford 1951) can be seen to work in exactly this way.

[47] The insufficient increase in the supply of certain agricultural products is due largely to the survival of numerous archaic peasant holdings, particularly in the South, and in some measure to the heavy protection of cereals. The development of the economy as a whole is affected by this shortfall, which pushes up the cost of living, causing wages to rise without any increase in the purchasing power of wage earners, and contributes to a rapid and continuous increase in food imports.

[48] Total exports remained stationary and industrial exports increased by only 3·4 per cent, as compared withh 17·1 per cent in 1956 and 18 per cent in 1957; world demand fell by more than 11 per cent.

[49] This rise was accelerated, via a sort of demonstration effect, by the pay increases granted by the government to public employees in 1962–63.

[50] See the author's 'Il problems dello sviluppo economico in Marx e in

57

Schumpeter' in *Economie capitalistiche ed economie pianificate*, Laterza, Bari 1960, p. 30.

[51] As I acknowledged in my article 'Relative prices and development programmes' *Banca nazionale del lavoro Quarterly Review* September 1957 and in the paper read to the National Research Council's study group (19 February 1965) entitled *Prezzi, salari, profitti e produttività in Italia dal 1951 al 1964*.

[52] Estimates made by A. Paolucci and included in the paper read to the National Research Council in 1965. The indices of productivity, production and earnings are set at 100 in the base year, industries are ranked in the final year and the rank coefficients calculated.

[53] The degree of concentration has been calculated using 1961 census data and Gini's method; *Informazioni SVIMEZ*, 24–31 March 1965.

[54] The divergence between the two coefficients is interesting. It might suggest that, in periods of sustained expansion, firms in which the growth of productivity is highest may set the pace for wage increases. In periods of less rapid expansion and of recession, on the other hand, union pressure is mainly responsible for wage increases and differentials between industries would tend to close, independently of present or past differences in productivity. See also section 8 above.

[55] The pressure of foreign competition is measured by the ratio of the value of imports to the value of domestic production.

[56] The equation is as follows (the *t* statistic is in brackets):

$$SH = -2139 \cdot 429 + 3 \cdot 856\, G + 1 \cdot 296\, SH_{us} + 14 \cdot 716\, \dot{L} \qquad R^2 = 0 \cdot 814$$
$$ (1 \cdot 712) \quad (6 \cdot 510) \qquad (2 \cdot 621)$$

where G is the share of industrial profits, SH_{us} is the index of United States share prices and $\dot{L}$ is the rate of change in total liquidity.

[57] '[The farmer's and manufacturer's] motive for accumulation will diminish with every diminution of profit, and will cease altogether when their profits are so low as not to afford them an adequate compensation for their trouble, and the risk which they must necessarily encounter in employing their capital productively' (D. Ricardo, *Principles*, Sraffa edition p. 122). It should be noted that Ricardo here touches on the notion of the 'minimum level of profit' which entered into our discussion of wage changes (section 8 above).

[58] With the classical economists, we may assume that in the past the cost of living affected wages in the long, not the short, period. They believed, realistically at the time, that wages *tended* to subsistence levels, but could fall even below such levels in the short period; unions either did not exist or were too weak to prevent this happening.

Appendix

Bibliography of selected empirical studies

1   Dow, J. C. R., and Dicks-Mireaux, L. A., 'The excess demand for labour' *Oxford Economic Papers,* February 1958.

2   Phillips, A. W., 'The relation between unemployment and the rate of change of money wage rates in the United Kingdom, 1861–1957' *Economica,* November 1958.

3   Dicks-Mireaux, L. A., and Dow, J. C.,R., 'The determinants of wage inflation: United Kingdom, 1946–1956'*Journal of the Royal Statistical Society,* 1959, pp. 145–83.

4   De Meo, G., 'Produttività e distribuzione del reddito in Italia nel periodo 1951–63' *Annali di statistica,* eight series, vol. 15, Istituto centrale di statistica, Rome 1965.

5   Klein, R. L., and Ball, J. R., 'Some econometrics on the determination of absolute prices and wages' *Economic Journal,* September 1959.

6   Lipsey, R. G., 'The relation between unemployment and the rate of change of money wage rates in the United Kingdom 1862–1957: a further analysis' *Economica,* February 1960.

7   Lipsey, R. G., and Steuer, M. D., 'The relation between profits and wage rates' *Economica* vol. 28, May 1961.

8   Neild, R. R., *Pricing and Employment in the Trade Cycle,* Cambridge University Press, 1963.

9   Kuh, E., 'Capital–stock growth: a microeconomic approach' Contributions to Economic Analysis XXXI, North Holland Publishing Press, 1964.

10   Meyer, J. R., and Glauber, R. R., *Investment Decisions, Economic Forecasting and Public Policy,* Boston 1964.

11   Dow, J. C. R., *The Management of the British Economy 1945–60,* Cambridge University Press, 1964.

12   Perry, G. L., *Unemployment, Money Wage Rates, and Inflation,* The MIT Press, Cambridge, Mass., 1966.

13   Rey, G. M., 'Una misura della capacità produttiva utilizzata nel settore industriale' *L'industria,* July–September 1965.

14   Kuh, E., 'A productivity theory of wage levels – an alternative to the Phillips curve' *Review of Economic Studies,* July 1967.

Statistical series and their sources

The basic data for observed (V_O) and estimated (V_E) values are shown at the bottom of each of the following charts, together with the figures calculated from the equations. For the other series and for the sources of all data, see my article 'Prezzi, distribuzione e investimenti in Italia dal 1951 al 1966: uno schema interpretativo' *Moneta e Credito*, September 1967.

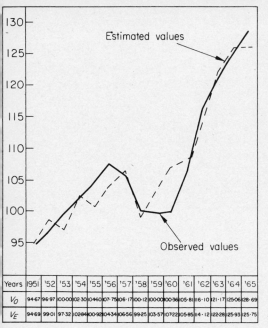

Years	1951	'52	'53	'54	'55	'56	'57	'58	'59	'60	'61	'62	'63	'64	'65
V_O	94·67	96·97	100·00	102·30	104·60	107·75	106·17	100·12	100·00	100·36	105·81	116·10	121·17	125·06	128·69
V_E	94·69	99·01	97·32	102·84	100·92	104·34	106·56	99·25	103·57	107·22	105·85	114·12	122·28	125·93	125·75

1. P_a – agricultural prices

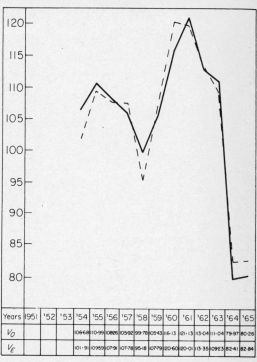

Years	1951	'52	'53	'54	'55	'56	'57	'58	'59	'60	'61	'62	'63	'64	'65
V_O				106·68	110·99	108·26	105·92	99·78	105·43	116·13	121·13	113·04	111·04	79·97	80·26
V_E				101·91	109·59	107·91	107·78	95·18	107·79	120·60	120·01	113·35	109·23	82·41	82·84

3. $\dot I$ – industrial investment

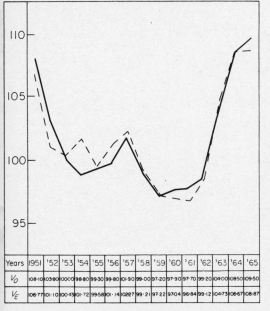

Years	1951	'52	'53	'54	'55	'56	'57	'58	'59	'60	'61	'62	'63	'64	'65
V_O	108·10	103·80	100·00	98·80	99·30	99·80	101·90	99·00	97·20	97·90	97·70	99·20	104·00	108·50	109·50
V_E	106·77	101·10	100·43	101·72	99·58	101·14	102·27	99·21	97·22	97·04	96·84	99·12	104·73	108·67	108·87

2. P_i – industrial prices

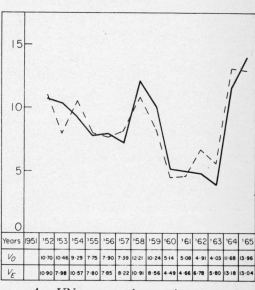

Years	1951	'52	'53	'54	'55	'56	'57	'58	'59	'60	'61	'62	'63	'64	'65
V_O		10·70	10·46	9·29	7·75	7·90	7·39	12·21	10·24	5·14	5·08	4·91	4·03	11·68	13·96
V_E		10·90	7·98	10·57	7·80	7·85	8·22	10·91	8·56	4·49	4·66	6·78	5·80	13·18	13·04

4. UN – unused capacity

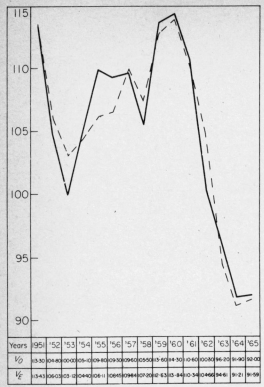

5. G – share of profits in manufacturing industry

Years	1951	'52	'53	'54	'55	'56	'57	'58	'59	'60	'61	'62	'63	'64	'65
V_O	113·30	104·80	100·00	105·10	109·80	109·30	109·60	105·50	113·60	114·30	110·60	100·30	96·20	91·90	92·00
V_E	113·43	106·03	103·12	104·40	106·11	106·45	109·84	107·20	112·63	113·84	110·34	104·66	94·61	91·21	91·59

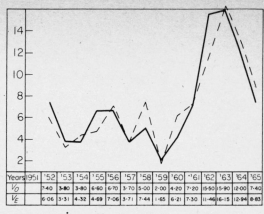

7. $\dot{W}_i$ – industrial wages

Years	1951	'52	'53	'54	'55	'56	'57	'58	'59	'60	'61	'62	'63	'64	'65
V_O		7·40	3·80	3·80	6·60	6·70	3·70	5·00	2·00	4·20	7·20	15·50	15·90	12·00	7·40
V_E		6·06	3·31	4·32	4·69	7·06	3·71	7·44	1·65	6·21	7·30	11·46	16·15	12·94	8·83

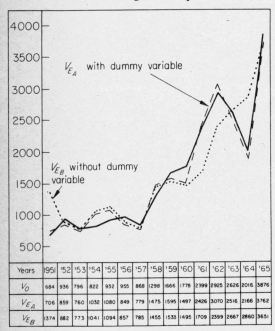

V_{E_A} with dummy variable

V_{E_B} without dummy variable

6. ΔL – total liquidity

Years	1951	'52	'53	'54	'55	'56	'57	'58	'59	'60	'61	'62	'63	'64	'65
V_O	684	936	796	822	932	955	868	1298	1666	1778	2399	2925	2626	2016	3876
V_{E_A}	706	859	760	1032	1080	849	779	1475	1595	1497	2426	3070	2516	2166	3762
V_{E_B}	1374	882	773	1041	1094	857	785	1455	1533	1495	1709	2399	2667	2860	3651

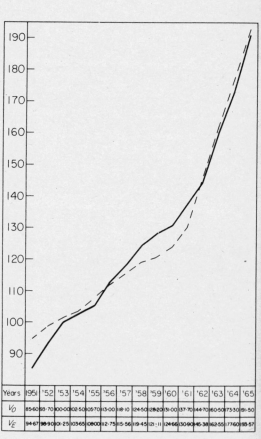

8. W_r – retail wages

Years	1951	'52	'53	'54	'55	'56	'57	'58	'59	'60	'61	'62	'63	'64	'65
V_O	85·60	93·70	100·00	102·50	105·70	113·00	118·10	124·50	128·20	131·00	137·70	144·70	160·50	173·30	191·50
V_E	94·67	98·90	101·25	103·65	108·00	112·75	115·56	119·45	121·11	124·66	130·90	145·38	162·55	177·60	193·57

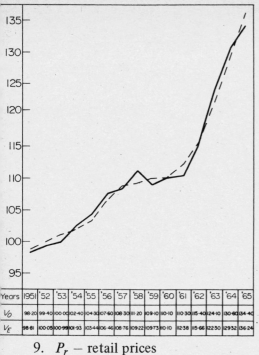

9. P_r – retail prices

Years	1951	'52	'53	'54	'55	'56	'57	'58	'59	'60	'61	'62	'63	'64	'65
V_O	98·20	99·40	100·00	102·40	104·30	107·60	108·30	111·20	109·10	110·10	110·30	115·40	124·10	130·60	134·40
V_E	98·61	100·05	100·99	101·93	103·44	106·46	108·76	109·22	109·73	110·10	112·38	115·66	122·30	129·32	136·24

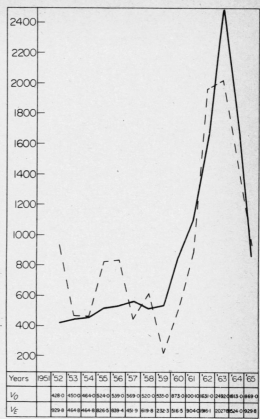

Years	1951	'52	'53	'54	'55	'56	'57	'58	'59	'60	'61	'62	'63	'64	'65
V_O		428·0	450·0	464·0	524·0	539·0	569·0	520·0	535·0	873·0	1001·0	1631·0	2492·0	1813·0	869·0
V_E		929·8	464·8	464·8	826·5	839·4	451·9	619·8	232·3	516·5	904·0	916·1	2027·8	1524·0	929·8

11. ΔR – dependent labour income

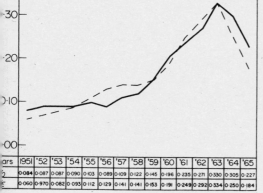

10. U^{-1} – non-agricultural employment (per cent)

Years	1951	'52	'53	'54	'55	'56	'57	'58	'59	'60	'61	'62	'63	'64	'65
V_O	0·084	0·087	0·087	0·090	0·103	0·089	0·109	0·122	0·145	0·196	0·235	0·271	0·330	0·305	0·227
V_E	0·060	0·070	0·082	0·093	0·112	0·129	0·141	0·153	0·191	0·249	0·292	0·334	0·250	0·184	

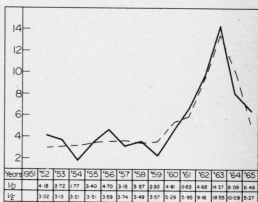

12. ΔC_v – private consumption

Years	1951	'52	'53	'54	'55	'56	'57	'58	'59	'60	'61	'62	'63	'64	'65
V_O		4·18	3·72	1·77	3·40	4·70	3·15	3·57	2·30	4·61	6·63	4·68	14·37	8·09	6·46
V_E		3·02	3·13	3·21	3·51	3·59	3·74	3·49	3·57	5·29	5·95	9·16	18·55	10·09	5·27

63

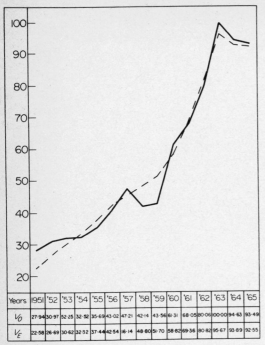

Years	1951	'52	'53	'54	'55	'56	'57	'58	'59	'60	'61	'62	'63	'64	'65
V_O	27·94	30·97	52·25	32·52	35·69	43·02	47·21	42·14	43·56	61·31	68·05	80·06	100·00	94·63	93·49
V_E	22·58	26·69	30·62	32·32	37·44	42·54	16·14	48·80	51·70	58·82	69·36	80·82	95·67	93·89	92·55

13. *IM* – imports

Years	1951	'52	'53	'54	'55	'56	'57	'58	'59	'60	'61	'62	'63	'64	'65
V_O	33·04	27·80	29·57	31·76	35·71	41·86	49·84	50·68	57·43	71·78	82·47	92·31	100·00	117·89	142·66
V_E	29·68	24·65	23·90	28·64	38·69	49·96	58·90	52·03	59·19	73·49	79·41	86·42	100·93	121·48	137·23

14. *E* – exports

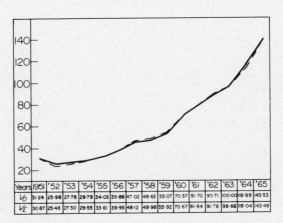

Years	1951	'52	'53	'54	'55	'56	'57	'58	'59	'60	'61	'62	'63	'64	'65
V_O	31·24	25·98	27·78	29·79	34·03	39·86	47·02	48·63	55·07	70·37	91·70	90·71	100·00	118·99	143·53
V_E	30·87	25·48	27·30	29·55	33·61	39·93	48·12	48·98	55·92	70·67	81·64	91·76	99·66	118·04	143·49

15. E_i – industrial exports

2 Market Forms, Trade Unions and Inflation

This chapter is divided into four parts. In the first part I consider the behaviour of prices in the short and long run in those market forms which are most relevant in modern conditions, that is, competition and oligopoly, competition being the rule in the primary producing activities, oligopoly in the others.

The second part deals with the labour market and with the forces which determine short-run and long-run changes in wages, with particular reference to the role of trade unions. I also try to present an overall view of the inflationary process. I consider very briefly the main sources of such a process; the external and internal limits which bring it to an end; the relations between the behaviour of prices and wages in the long run, and the role of variations in effective demand, both in the short and in the long run.

In the third part, I present certain empirical findings which seem to support the propositions set forth in the previous parts. In particular, it appears that the elasticity of prices with respect to direct cost is less than unity in the short run and tends to unity in the long run. As for wages, the role of the trade unions in the short run can be detected by using, as an index of the unions' 'pushfulness', the number of hours lost through strikes; in the long run, it seems that the growth of trade unions has modified the very structure of the wage equation. A few data are presented at the end, concerning the behaviour of productivity and prices during periods of inflation.

In the last part, some of the main international factors affecting prices and wages are briefly discussed.

I Competition and oligopoly

1 *Competition*

'It is the cost of production which must ultimately regulate the price of commodities, and not, as has often been said, the proportion between the supply and demand: the proportion between supply and demand may, indeed, for a time, affect the market value of a commodity, until it is supplied in greater or less abundance, according as the demand may have increased or diminished; but this effect will be only of temporary duration'.[1] These propositions by David Ricardo imply competitive conditions, that is, free entry, and remain valid today in those areas of the economy where such conditions still exist. In the short run, then, in competitive markets prices depend on supply and demand, whereas in the long run they depend on total average cost.

Agriculture is one of the few areas of the economy where competition still exists. Let us call P_a the index of agricultural prices, S the index of the supply of agricultural products, and let us take C_v, total demand for consumer goods at current prices, as an indicator of the change in demand for agricultural products. Let us write

$$AC = \alpha \frac{W_a}{\pi_a} + \beta M_a + \theta \frac{k}{x}$$

where AC is an index of average cost for agricultural products, W_a wages per man, π_a output per man, M_a the price of goods and services bought by farmers, and α and β appropriate weights for the cost of labour (W_a/π_a) and the cost of goods and services.

We may use yearly data for the short-run relation and a three- or four-year moving average for the long-run relation. Neglecting fixed cost and writing, respectively, $P_{a(s)}$ and $P_{a(l)}$ for the two relations, we have

$$P_{a(s)} = a - bS + cC_v \qquad (2.1)$$

and

$$P_{a(l)} = \alpha' \frac{W_a}{\pi_a} + \beta' M_a \qquad (2.2)$$

These relations may hold good not only for agricultural prices but also for the prices of raw materials, with two important qualifications. In most Western countries there is a floor to variations in the prices of certain agricultural products, owing to price support policies followed by governments and implemented in various ways. The same applies to the prices of certain raw materials, owing to government intervention or to formal or tacit agreements among firms. When there is only a floor to variations of prices, the competitive model can hold good, with the proviso that a minimum level has to be taken into account.[2] When prices are controlled by means of monopolistic or oligopolistic agreements, then that model no longer applies.

In modern industry oligopolistic conditions prevail, that is, entry is not free but there are obstacles of various kinds and at different levels. In industries with a dominant and relatively homogeneous product (e.g. steel), the main barrier to entry depends, *given the size of the market*, on the minimum size necessary to carry out production at competitive costs; this is the 'technological barrier'. In industries where product differentiation prevails, the main barrier to entry is given by the large commercial and promotional expenditures necessary for a firm to break into the market and then to expand, or at least to maintain its market share; this is the 'commercial barrier'. Commercial and promotional expenditures partake of the characteristics of fixed cost; the larger they are the larger output must be, in order to have a tolerably low cost per unit, quite apart from technological reasons. Again, the size of the market makes the commercial barrier more or less effective. Many, perhaps most, non-durable consumer goods industries belong to this category. I have called 'homogeneous' or 'concentrated' oligopoly the market situation where the technological barrier is particularly relevant, 'differentiated' or 'imperfect' oligopoly the market situation where the commercial barrier prevails, and 'mixed' oligopoly the situation in which we find a combination of the two types of barriers (most durable consumer goods and the engineering industries belong in this category).

Given the size of the market, the different barriers give rise to different rates of profit; and since the barriers operate with different intensities within each industry, firms operating in each industry obtain on the average different rates of profit, even when considering a relatively long period.

Under such conditions, supply is administered in order to administer prices. When demand falls, output is reduced correspondingly in order to keep the price stable; when demand expands, output, as a rule, is increased correspondingly. Usually firms, especially the largest among them, keep unused capacity in hand for meeting short-run (seasonal or cyclical) expansion of demand; they calculate standard costs, which they use as the basis for administering prices, with reference to the standard volume of production, which is greater than the output corresponding to the break-even point but less than the output corresponding to full capacity. Moreover, large firms build capacity ahead of demand, i.e. they anticipate, by means of market studies, the probable long-run expansion of demand, not only because the gestation period of investment is often relatively long, but also because they intend to use their unused capacity as a deterrent for potential new entrants. As a result, in the short run prices depend on the behaviour of cost, although they do not vary in the same proportion; only in special circumstances, that is, when the actual expansion of demand is considerably greater than the expected expansion, and full capacity is reached in most firms, does demand contribute to price variations (increases).

In a given situation, the size of the market, the elasticity of demand for the whole industry and the barriers to entry explain the *level* of price; the differential effects of the barriers to entry, owing to technological and commercial economies of scale, explain the different levels of cost of different firms (costs of production + commercial costs). Given the price and the cost level, the largest firms which, as a rule, act as price leaders, use the margin between price and cost ('mark-up') to change prices when market conditions vary, particularly when cost varies as a consequence of changes in the price of inputs. In other words, the so-called full-cost principle, which is meaningless when referred to the analytical problem of price determination, becomes meaningful when referred to the problem of price variations; its rationale appears, not in a static, but in a dynamic context.

Let us now consider manufacturing industry, which is the most important and most dynamic industrial subsector. For an empirical analysis of variations in the prices of manufactured goods in the short run, we may use the following relation:

$$P_{i(s)} = a + b \frac{W_i}{\pi_i} + cM_i \qquad (2.3)$$

where $W_i/\pi_i = L_i$ is the cost of labour. In terms of rates of change, we can write

$$\dot{P}_{i(s)} = \gamma \dot{L}_i + \delta \dot{M}_i. \qquad (2.3a)$$

The sum of the two coefficients $(\gamma+\delta)$ expresses the elasticity of price with respect to direct cost.[3] If the mark-up were constant, we would have $\gamma+\delta = 1$. But the mark-up is not constant in each period (each year); it tends to be constant only in the long run, over a number of years. One reason for this is that when average direct cost increases because of an increase in wages larger than the average increase in productivity (output per man-hour) and/or an increase in the price of raw materials, the increase is not distributed evenly throughout the economy. The most dynamic firms, which are often the largest, are able to offset the increase in the price of variable factors by raising productivity at the same rate. Such firms, however, may also decide not to raise their prices in the same proportion as direct cost because they want to avoid discouraging the expansion of demand and because they intend to obtain higher profit margins when direct cost decreases (mainly as a result of productivity rising more rapidly than wages). The less dynamic firms either succeed in increasing their productivity in the long run, or are eliminated – they are absorbed by more dynamic firms or go bankrupt. Moreover, when average direct cost increases, the firms which act as price leaders may refrain from shifting the cost increases fully onto prices for fear of foreign competition (increase in imports and/or decrease in exports), assuming that in the market of other industrial countries prices are not rising or rising only at a moderate rate.

For these and other reasons, in the short run the average increase in direct cost is not fully reflected in higher prices. (Incidentally, this may help to explain why, in our times, during periods of inflation the average rate of profit often goes down, whereas in the past rising prices were associated with decreasing profits only in the final stage of a boom).

When average direct cost goes down, prices as a rule do not fall in the same proportion, because the most dynamic firms are not compelled by foreign competition to reduce prices that much, nor do they find it expedient to reduce prices in the same proportion as their specific direct cost. They reduce them only to the extent to which they deem it necessary to prevent the entry of other firms; and since the innovations that they are able to introduce are not always readily accessible to other firms, they can be fairly sure that the rise in profit margins will create no risk of their markets being invaded, at least in the short run. Moreover, since the major firms which act as price leaders are aiming at a certain rate of return not in every single year, but over a number of years, the higher profit margins obtained when direct cost decreases are intended to compensate for the lower margins in years of rising direct cost.[4]

In the short run the elasticity of prices with respect to direct cost is less than unity, but in the long run it tends to become equal to unity, i.e. costs and prices tend to vary in the same proportion, both because the major firms deliberately follow this policy and because the less dynamic firms either succeed in offsetting the increase in the prices of variable factors or else disappear. It is to be noted that in the long run the changes in the cost of home-produced raw materials fully reflect changes in labour cost, so that it is the elasticity of prices with respect to labour cost which tends to approach unity, unless, in the country considered, the relative weight of imported raw materials is significant.

Granted that short-run prices vary with costs, but not in the same proportion, one should not think that rising costs and prices are mechanically associated with cyclical upswings, and falling costs and prices with cyclical downswings. Costs rise either because of an increase in the prices of raw materials (including agricultural commodities) or because wage rises outpace productivity gains. Agricultural and raw material prices are sensitive to variations of demand, which follow a quasi-cyclical pattern; but wages vary with a delay, because they depend to a considerable extent on collective bargaining, which takes place at relatively long intervals. As a consequence, wages may well continue to rise in a downswing, thus pushing industrial prices up. On the other hand, as several economists have pointed out, the increasing amount of capital per man and the increasing employment of skilled personnel and technicians lead to a decreasing propensity of firms to dismiss workers and employees when demand and output are shrinking; this means that when demand goes down, the rate of increase in output per man-hour also goes down, and this causes additional upward pressure on costs and therefore on prices.

Finally, big firms, which are often price leaders, make their decisions with reference to a long time-horizon. One consequence of this is that they change their prices with a view to obtaining a target rate of return over a number of years. Another consequence is that investment programmes are prepared well in advance and investment expenditure becomes relatively rigid with respect to short-term variations in demand and in profits.

Considering all these factors, one can easily understand why industrial prices and even investment may continue to go up during a recession for quite a long while (say, one year or more), or may remain relatively stable during an upswing or even at the beginning of a boom.

The above factors also help to explain why industrial prices have become increasingly rigid with respect to demand. There are, however, exceptions to this kind of rigidity, which are to be found in extreme situations, that is, situations approaching competition (e.g. textiles) or situations approaching monopoly (e.g. local monopolies, protected by high costs of transportation; or national monopolies, when there are high barriers to foreign competition). In such situations demand does affect industrial prices, at least in the short run.

3   International oligopolies

What has been said for industrial oligopolies applies, as a rule, to home markets, which are to some extent protected from foreign competition by customs duties, costs of transportation and by what can be dubbed 'hidden protection', that is, control of commercial channels and first-hand knowledge of administrative laws, regulations and practices.

However, owing to the progressive reduction of the above barriers, international oligopolies are nowadays emerging in an increasing number of industries, or indeed are already in effect. Cases in point are steel, oil, glass, certain basic chemicals, cars, tyres, computers and electronic machines. Here we find, at the international level, price leadership and several other characteristic features of oligopolistic behaviour. With some form of tacit agreement or collusion among the main producers, price variations have to be explained with reference to market conditions not in a single market but in the markets of all the industrial countries. When in one such industry capacity is fully or almost fully utilised, not in one given country but in all the countries concerned, then demand expansion can help to explain a price rise which might not have occurred had full capacity been reached in one country only. In such a situation that country's main producers would be unable to meet the demand of their customers, whether or not the price has been raised. If the price has not been raised, unfilled orders will accumulate, but only the customers with urgent needs will turn to foreign producers; if the price has been raised, unfilled orders will not increase and the higher price will 'clear the (home) market', but the firms concerned may well permanently lose some customers to their competitors. If competitors abroad have unused capacity, then the most advantageous line of action is *not* to raise the price (that is, *not* to maximise short-run profits), but if these competitors have also reached full capacity, then there are no more obstacles to raising the price. One of the producers may act as price leader; the others will follow.[5]

4 *Market conditions in retail trade, services and housing*

In retail trade, locational and commercial imperfections restrict competition within rather small circles of tradesmen, so that differentiated or imperfect oligopoly appears to be the most common market form. In recent decades, especially in the large towns of the most advanced countries, large commercial units (department and chain stores, supermarkets) entered the retail market, at least for certain categories of goods; as a result retail margins narrowed. The market forms characterised by the new large commercial units can best be described as approximating concentrated oligopoly. Large units can do much more than small ones to increase the efficiency of labour in retail trade; this is one reason for the reduction in retail margins − not by a once and for all change, but by a gradual process. A more potent reason is what we may call the innovating process by which large units gain a rapidly expanding market share at the expense of small ones. In order to survive, the small units try to take shelter in geographical and commercial areas where large units cannot compete. When some form of equilibrium is achieved between large and small businesses in retail trade, further gains in labour efficiency become more difficult to obtain (efficiency being expressed by the ratio between the volume of consumer goods sold in a given period and the number of workers employed).

The main difference between the small and large commercial units consists in the degree and the rate of change of efficiency; when they compete more or less directly, small firms must accept the price leadership of larger units, since the latter have more efficiency and are in a position to sell a much larger variety of goods. In 'sheltered' areas small units enjoy some market power and can directly influence retail prices.

All things considered, price behaviour in retail trade can be expected to be similar to that in industrial oligopolistic markets. The criterion followed by the commercial units with market power can be assumed to be that of 'target mark-up' pricing (because of the relatively small amount of fixed capital in retail trade, it seems reasonable to assume that price leaders do not follow the second, more refined criterion of pricing). There is, however, at least one difference between the behaviour of retail prices of commodities and that of wholesale industrial prices: foreign competition does not exert any direct pressure on the former. For this and other reasons, which need not be discussed in this context, we can assume that retailers are in a position to shift increases in their costs entirely onto consumers; this means that the elasticity of prices with respect to direct commercial costs is equal to unity, even in the short run. For the retailer the main cost elements are the prices of products at the wholesale stage and the cost of labour, that is, the ratio between wages and the 'efficiency' of labour (defined as above). If wholesale prices are constant but the efficiency of labour in retail trade increases less than wages, the cost of labour goes up and retail prices increase; they increase even more when wholesale prices rise. This appears to be what has been happening, so that the gap between wholesale and retail prices of commodities has been gradually widening in most Western countries.

The case of housing is one where we have typically imperfect markets into which foreign competition does not enter at all. The production costs of the building industry and the prices of building sites exert the main influence on the variations of house prices. In most countries the cost of production in building activities have shown a tendency to rise even when wholesale industrial prices were relatively stable; the fact is that productivity both in the industries producing building materials and in construction increases less than the average, since these industries, at least until now, have not been able to introduce mass production methods. The price of building sites, which depends on the speed of urbanisation, tends to increase, except at times of recession. In consequence rents, which are an important item in the cost of living, tend to increase almost without interruption. Prices of services, on the other hand, and especially personal services, tend to increase in proportion to the increase in wages and salaries paid in industry.

All this means that, if wholesale prices are stable, the prices of consumer goods and services go up, thus pushing wages up regardless of productivity gains. Prices of consumer goods and services would remain stable under two conditions: (1) wholesale prices decline, thus causing a (smaller) decline in retail prices of commodities; (2) prices of services (including rents) go up only to the extent of matching the decline in the retail prices of commodities. As we shall see, it is very unlikely, except in special circumstances, that these conditions might ever obtain nowadays.

II Trade unions, prices and wages

5 *Wages and productivity in the short run*

Price behaviour in industry and trade, both in the short and in the long run, is governed by cost behaviour, whereas price behaviour for many agricultural products and raw materials is governed by cost behaviour only in the long run. Labour is the main cost element. We have, then, to consider how wages change in the short and the long run and concentrate the analysis on wages in manufacturing industry, if we assume that this is the most dynamic sector of the economy, from which, as a rule, the main impulses propagate to the rest of the system.[6]

Trade unions find it easier to obtain wage increases in those industries where (a) productivity rises faster than the average and/or (b) the leading firms possess relatively strong market power. Very often, the two conditions are found together, especially in highly concentrated industries.

There is no doubt, then, that productivity variations affect wage variations; but the opposite also holds good. If it is true that firms which are able to obtain above-average productivity increases are more willing to grant wage increases, it is also true that, when trade unions succeed in getting substantial wage rises, *as a consequence* all the laggard firms try to raise productivity in order to offset the higher wages. On the other hand, firms do not try to offset higher wages only in this way; they also try to achieve the same result by raising prices. It is not easy to disentangle these relations, where a given element from one standpoint is a 'cause' and from another an 'effect'.

In the short run (one year) it is clearly unreasonable to imagine that productivity would vary in response to a variation in wages; in the short run, productivity changes are to be considered as an exogenous variable, at least with respect to wages. (Productivity changes may be correlated with changes in employment, but this is another question.)

As we have seen, there are good reasons to believe that in the short run industrial prices are affected by productivity changes, according to the equation

$$P_{i(s)} = a + b \frac{W_i}{\pi_i} + cM_i.$$

On the basis of this relation, we might also take as formally valid a function of the type

$$W_i = f(P_{i(s)} \, \pi_i) \tag{2.3b}$$

where, for simplicity, raw material prices are omitted. Whether or not the statistical fits are good, such an equation cannot be used to 'explain' short-run variations in industrial wages, unless we assume (which I think would be wrong) that in the short run not only productivity but also wholesale industrial prices are independent of wages.[7] The equation, then, cannot be used to explain short-run wage variations.

On the other hand, we might be justified in taking a function of the type

$$W_i = \phi(\pi_i)$$

since in the short run changes in productivity could be taken as an independent variable with respect to wages. A function of this type has in fact been considered by certain economists, but few have denied that other factors as well contribute to determine wage variations in the short run. Among these other factors we find the tension in the labour market, expressed by the degree of unemployment or by some variant of it, the rate of change in the cost of living and the degree of unionisation, which is supposed to express the 'pushfulness' of the trade unions.

6 Short-run variations in wages

'The general movements of wages are exclusively regulated by the expansion and contraction of the industrial reserve army, and these again correspond to the periodic changes of the industrial cycle'.[8]

It would be difficult to express the 'Phillips relation', i.e. the relation between short-run wage variations and unemployment, more effectively than Marx did in the above proposition.

From the painstaking empirical enquiries by Phillips and Lipsey it appears that up to the beginning of this century, or to the first world war, short-run wage variations were explained largely by the degree of unemployment and its variations. It seems that only in the last five or six decades the cost of living became another important explanatory variable. This can be accounted for by the fact that only when trade unions have become strong enough and collective bargaining has become a widely recognised method for varying the general (minimum) level of wages, does the cost of living become one of the factors for explaining the short-run variations of wages.[9] In countries like Italy, where escalator clauses are included in all labour contracts, the relation between wage changes and cost-of-living changes is obvious. Even the introduction of the escalator clause is a result of the pressure of trade unions and of political parties representing labour interests. Moreover, in collective bargaining trade union leaders take into account the trend of prices, even apart from the escalator clause which applies to contractual wages and therefore can guarantee only a part of the workers' real earnings.

Productivity, too, can be counted among the factors explaining short-run wage changes only when trade unions have become strong enough, for while it is true that firms which are able to obtain above-average productivity gains are willing to pay higher wages, they do as a rule (though not necessarily) need a 'push' to do so.

It is not at all certain a priori, however, that productivity, that is, physical output per man-hour, really does contribute to wage determination in the short run. Moreover, when we say that the most dynamic firms are apt to grant the highest wage increases, we refer to a process which should be analysed in disaggregated and not in aggregated (average) terms.[10] It is true that, via spillover and demonstration effects, the higher wages granted by a restricted number of firms (or industries) gradually push up other wages as well. But we cannot be certain that such effects will materialise in the short period. In Italy, productivity proved to add relatively little to the statistical explanation of wage movements, whereas it seems to have more significance when we make a disaggregated analysis and consider a period of several years (see section 18 below.)[11]

7 The short-run effects of trade union action

In an historical perspective, one of the main effects of unions, from the narrow point of view of the conditions in the labour market, is to introduce a new term into the original Marxian relation; instead of

$$\dot{W} = f(U) \tag{2.4a}$$

we have, in modern conditions,

$$\dot{W} = \phi(U, \dot{V}) \tag{2.4b}$$

where $\dot{W}$ is the rate of change in wages, U is the percentage of unemployment and $\dot{V}$ the rate of change in the cost of living. [12] This relation 'explains' a good part of the variance of wage changes, in Italy as well as in many other countries. [13]

The growth of trade unions, then, has had the consequence of modifying the basic wage equation. We might expect, however, that trade union pressure would exert also a direct influence. Several indices of union 'pushfulness' have been devised, but, to my knowledge, nobody has yet tried to use the number of man-hours (or man-days) lost owing to strikes. I did so and the results were positive: in Italy the addition of such a variable not only increases the explanatory power of the wage equation, but considerably improves the fit for the whole period considered (see section 17 below). We have, then, a third function

$$\dot{W} = F(U, \dot{V}, TUP) \tag{2.4c}$$

where TUP is trade union pressure, quantified according to the number of man-hours lost through strikes, and where trade union influence appears indirectly in the $\dot{V}$ variable and directly in the TUP variable.

8 The long-run effects of wage increases on productivity and employment

Whereas in the short run productivity is to be considered as independent of wages, we might expect that in the long run it will to some extent be affected by wage variations. In particular we might expect that above-normal wage increases will induce firms to step up productivity gains by introducing labour-saving investment (I am referring only to manufacturing industry). This is mainly because, as we have seen, in the short run firms can shift only part of direct cost increases onto prices. More precisely, firms in which productivity is already rising rapidly can at once fully offset an increase in wages, but the less dynamic firms may succeed in doing so only with a delay; they are nevertheless stimulated, or compelled, to reorganise and raise productivity more rapidly than before.

A priori, we cannot say confidently whether the effect we are considering can be detected statistically, since the factors which influence productivity changes are very complex. In Italy, we made several experiments to test the relation between wages and productivity in the long run, but the results were not conclusive. We also tried to test a second proposition, namely, whether an above-normal wage increase influences in the opposite direction the rate of change in employment by stimulating labour-saving investment. The empirical test of this proposition gave more favourable results (see section 18 below).

To offset the impact of wage increases, firms not only have the possibility of speeding up the rise in productivity, but they can also raise prices; and this, as we have seen, is the main reaction in the short run, since productivity cannot be modified rapidly.

The transfer of cost increases onto prices depends not only on the behaviour of individual firms, but also on conditions throughout the whole economic system. In certain conditions prices rises will be general and cumulative; that is, an inflationary process will take place. The transfer onto prices of wage increases in excess of 'normal' productivity gains will then be cumulative. It must be added that, in such conditions, increases in productivity, far from being promoted, are discouraged. The fact is that the inflationary process stimulates speculative investment to the detriment of productive investment. Moreover, with a high and increasing degree of capacity utilisation, less efficient plant will be put into operation, and with a high and increasing level of employment, workers with below-average skill will be hired. At the same time raw material prices rise and thus help to push up direct cost. As we know, each increase in direct cost is shifted only partially onto prices and the price increase will fall more and more behind the cost increase. This latter will become more and more rapid, for three reasons: wage increases, below-average increases in productivity and increases in the price of raw materials. As a consequence, the average rate of profit will tend to fall. Only when the cost-push has slowed down will firms be able to restore profit margins, chiefly by speeding up productivity gains. In such conditions prices — I mean wholesale prices — will stop rising or even show a (mildly) falling trend.

All things considered, in the long run the increases in money wages and in the average *value* productivity (the index of output per man-hour multiplied by the index of wholesale prices of industrial products) will tend to coincide. This relation, however, cannot be interpreted in a simple causal way, since the two variables interact with one another. Perhaps, in the long run, money wages have a predominantly active role with respect to average value productivity, that is, with respect to prices *and* to physical productivity.

9   *Trade unions, prices and the distribution of income*

Granted that trade unions have the power to influence variations in money wages, the next question is whether they have an influence on real wages as well, and whether they can alter the distribution of income in favour of wage earners.

On the point of income distribution a definite answer can be given only in the case of industry, where paid workers predominate. In agriculture and in retail trade self-employed labour is very common, [14] at least in an economy like Italy's.

In the short period, as we have seen, a rise in direct cost is associated with a less than proportional increase in industrial prices (the elasticity of price with respect to direct cost is considerably less than unity). It follows that to the extent that trade unions influence wages, they influence also the distribution of industrial income. It is simply not true, as some economists maintain, that industrial capitalists are in a position to thwart the unions' wage claims by shifting onto prices the full increase in labour costs (the ratio of wages and productivity), for the unions do have effective power — which they can use for better or for worse — both to influence wages and in broader political terms. If it were not so it would be hard to understand why not only economic policy makers are usually in favour of an incomes policy, but industrial capitalists as well.

In the long run the direct-cost elasticity of prices tends towards unity. Hence, in the long run, the distribution of industrial income between wages and profits tends to remain fairly stable, provided the capital/output ratio in its turn keeps relatively stable. However, it may happen that a short-period increase in the wages share becomes, in part, durable — in which case the subsequent long-period stability occurs at a higher level. [15] Furthermore wage increases, especially those which in the short period exceed productivity gains, have an effect on income growth and on productivity gains as such. Productivity can be regarded as independent of wages only in the short period; in the long period those firms which cannot pay higher labour costs disappear, and the remaining firms speed up productivity gains. It follows that trade union action, while largely (but not wholly) neutral in the long period so far as income distribution is concerned, is not neutral with respect to the growth (or the composition) of income itself, as well as to productivity increases. [16]

All this applies only to industry and to the two distributive shares of wages and profits (gross profits, including interest). But what about rent?

In the capitalist industrial countries, the farm rent has been tending to fall in relative (and perhaps even in absolute) terms. But, with growing urbanisation in the wake of industrialisation, the rent of building sites has been growing. This increasing locational rent has been driving up the rents and prices of dwellings well beyond their, likewise rising, construction costs. Rapidly rising rents hold back the increase in the purchasing power of wages, and, by pushing up both the cost of living and money wages, also add to the pace of cost increases in industry. To this extent they have been, and still are, restraining the process of growth, in much the same way as land rent does in Ricardo's argument.[17]

There remains the question as to whether trade unions have any influence on changes in real wages. In Italy, as in other industrial countries, real wages have in recent decades been rising less than money wages, because the cost of living has been going up even at stationary wholesale prices and, at times of increasing wholesale prices, has outpaced them. There are three main reasons why the cost of living keeps outpacing wholesale prices: higher gross retail margins, the rising price of personal and real services, and rising rents. Retail price margins rise because efficiency gains in retail trade are not enough to offset increases in the pay of shop assistants. Much the same applies to services. Part of the productivity gains in the production of goods thus accrues to those who work in retail trade and the services. As for rents, their increase is largely due to the higher economic rent of building sites.

The important point to remember, then, is that the cost of living is driven up not only by rising wages, but also by other factors, the chief of which are the slowness, even in the long period, of efficiency gains in retail trade, and rising rents.

To the extent that autonomous trade union action succeeds in pushing money wages up ahead of the rise in the cost of living (which would occur in any case) and thus widening the gap between the two, trade unions do in effect influence real wages as well.

In addition, of course, trade union action indirectly affects the volume and composition of investment, and thereby ultimately the whole process of economic growth.

10   The inflationary process: an overall view

So far we have been considering individual sectors of the economy — the markets for several categories of goods and services and the labour market. Now let us look at the economy as a whole and examine, in particular, how an inflationary process is generated, and what 'objective' forces and policy decisions may bring it to an end. To make the transition from partial to general analysis we would need a model for the whole economy, possibly capable of being converted into an econometric model susceptible of empirical verification.

I do not propose to do this here. Instead, my purposes will be served well enough by the simplified econometric model for the Italian economy presented in Chapter 1. I will briefly indicate some of the main theoretical propositions on which this model rests, and which were supported (I do not venture to say 'proved') by empirical findings.

An inflationary process in any given country may be of domestic or of international origin. Its origin is domestic when, in the last analysis, it is generated either by a private investment boom or by an expansion of public expenditure (especially when this expansion occasions a budget deficit), or by both — subject to the proviso that even then inflation occurs only on certain conditions. One of these conditions is that the banking system is willing to finance (directly or indirectly) the private or the public sector by increasing the money supply. In other words, an increase in the money supply is not in itself, and cannot be, the 'cause' of inflation. Inflation is 'caused' by decision centres — by the spending decisions of private firms or government. Take the case of inflation due to deficit spending by government. If, in disregard of this fact, certain economists insist that the money supply should be reduced, they are saying, in effect, that no new taxes should be imposed in order to eliminate the budget deficit (which is inflating the money supply), and advocating a cut in the credits which finance private investment. It is clearly misleading, then, to talk of the money supply in abstract terms, without reference to the decision centres responsible for spending.

In addition to the policy of the banking system, one or both of the following conditions must be met for inflation to occur. The degree of unemployment must be relatively low, and/or there must be an increase in the demand for goods the supply of which is rigid at least in the short run. In the former case, inflation is predominantly of the 'cost-push' type, that is, predominantly due to wage increases; in the second case, inflation is mainly of the 'demand-pull' type. The two conditions can, and most often do, combine; but analytically they have to be treated separately.[18] Industry and trade are the typical areas of cost-push inflation, mining and agriculture those of demand-pull inflation.[19] (This implies, among other things, that a fall in industrial and a rise in agricultural prices, or *vice versa*, may occur simultaneously). Since the cost of living tends to rise even at stable wholesale prices — because of the relatively slow increase in the efficiency of retail trade and of increases in rents and the prices of services — and since a rise in the cost of living pushes up wages regardless of increases in output per man and of the state of the labour market, the cost of living must be regarded as a force contributing to structural cost-push inflation.

An inflationary process is of international origin when it is generated by an increase in the prices of imported raw materials, in which case it takes the form of cost-push inflation at home, or in those of finished products, in which case the domestic effect is an upward shift of the limit to price increases for domestic products or, more directly, an increase in the prices of imported finished products.

Domestic and international inflationary pressures often combine; more precisely, the former may work independently of the latter, while international pressures are translated into domestic ones when their effects work through beyond the first link in the causal chain.

But regardless of what, in the first instance, causes prices to rise, they tend to go on doing so via a price—wage spiral. Where are the limits to such a process?

There is an internal and an external limit. The internal limit works in the following way. Profit margins are gradually eroded, mainly because in the short run cost increases are only in part transformed into price increases, but also because, in a period of protracted inflation, the rate of increase in productivity tends to slow down. The fall in profits holds back the growth of private investment, both because the volume of self-financing declines and because the incentive to invest is blunted. The lower rate of increase, or the lower level, of investment causes unemployment to go up and the rate of increase in wages to slow down; hence the upward pressure on non-competitive prices is reduced. Both the increase in unemployment and the decrease in wage rises cause a reduction in the rate of increase, or the absolute level, of the wage fund, thus reducing the consumers' expenditure, or its rate of increase. The reduction of producers' and consumers' expenditure lessens the pressure of demand throughout the economy, including those markets where such lower pressure may lead to a fall in prices.

The external limit depends on the balance of payments. With home demand expanding rapidly and home prices rising, imports are accelerated and exports decelerated. The balance on goods and services deteriorates. Sooner or later, this deterioration is reflected in a deterioration of the balance of payments. This tends to slow down liquidity creation unless the central bank takes countermeasures; the volume of bank credit tends to fall and the ensuing credit squeeze discourages private investment. In consequence, unemployment goes up and the rate of increase in wages and prices moderates. Prolonged balance-of-payments deterioration causes a fall in gold and foreign exchange reserves. If, in such a situation, the central bank does not try to offset the automatic tendency of bank credit to shrink, but, using its discretionary power, restricts the money supply — that is, the availability of credit — then investment expenditure must fall. The consequences are the same as those discussed above, including a contraction of demand for producer goods. Since prices stop rising and home demand is stagnant, producers concentrate on export sales, and as a result the balance on goods and services improves.

Without taking this kind of analysis any further, I should merely like to add a few comments on the economy of the United States. Of the three inflationary processes in the US since the end of the war — 1950–51, 1955–58 and 1964–70 — only the second can be attributed to an investment boom; the first and the third were clearly generated by a particularly rapid expansion of public expenditure, especially military spending (Korean war, Vietnam war), although private investment, too, was stimulated on both occasions by military spending. The trouble with the American economy is that both limits which bring the inflationary process to an end are much less effective than in other advanced countries. When profit margins and self-financing fall, the big American corporations are able to obtain funds either through their foreign subsidiaries or on money markets abroad (especially Europe). Bank credit restrictions are, to a certain extent and for some time, circumvented in the same way. And American economic policy makers feel much less compelled than their colleagues in other advanced countries to introduce fiscal and monetary restrictive measures, since the dollar is generally used as a reserve currency and a balance-of-payments deficit can safely go on for years — as indeed it has been doing, thus swelling the dollar reserves of other countries. So long as the dollar was linked with gold, their mounting reserves made it easier for other countries to pursue a cheap money policy and thus indirectly added to inflationary pressure; a similar result followed from attempts to use the national currency to prop up the value of the dollar reserves. After the dollar was officially cut loose from gold and subsequently devalued, international inflationary pressure emanating from the United States became much stronger, especially as regards raw material prices quoted in dollars.

11 *The long-run behaviour of prices and wages: comparison between the nineteenth and the twentieth century*

As is well known, during the greater part of the last century industrial prices showed a falling trend; agricultural and raw material prices declined, too, but less rapidly, so that the 'terms of trade' between the two sectors moved in favour of agriculture and the production of raw materials (I refer to English and American statistical data). Apart from temporary (cyclical) setbacks, national income rose throughout the whole century; it rose no less and sometimes even more rapidly during periods in which prices were falling than during the (much shorter) periods of rising prices.

By contrast, in our century both industrial and agricultural prices have shown a tendency to rise, especially after the second world war. During the interwar period prices fell sharply between 1929 and 1933 and recovered their 1929 level only at the outbreak of the war. In the same period, however, contrary to what happened in the last century at times of falling prices, national income and especially industrial output fell much more sharply than prices. Agricultural prices fell much more than industrial ones, whereas agricultural output did not decline at all. In our century we have no instances of prolonged price falls accompanied by a rise in industrial output, and the terms of trade between primary products and industrial products have, until recently, moved against the former.

We have seen that, in the long run, prices depend on costs both under competitive and under oligopolistic conditions. Are market forms then a matter of indifference with regard to the long-run behaviour of prices? Oligopoly has become the prevalent market form in industrial markets only in our century, mainly in consequence of the rapid process of concentration which started towards the end of the last century, gathered momentum at the turn of the century and since then has been continuing, though at a slower pace. Why then, in our times, does the behaviour of prices differ so profoundly from what it was in the nineteenth century?

Let us consider, first, the industrial sector before the growth of corporations and the beginning of the modern process of concentration. In those days, individual firms were the rule and they were unable to influence prices; in order to obtain increasing profits they tried to reduce costs, mainly by introducing new machinery. In principle, when labour input is reduced, money cost also diminishes, provided that money wages do not change or increase less than productivity. In fact, money wages remained approximately stable in the first half of the nineteenth century, whereas in the second half they increased systematically less than productivity. As long as the supply of labour was economically unlimited and such trade unions as there were had little bargaining power, the 'masters' succeeded in keeping money wages stable or in restraining their increase, since they were strong in the labour market and the workmen were weak. Adam Smith described this situation very well:

The masters, being fewer in number, can combine much more easily; and the law, besides, authorises, or at least does not prohibit their combinations, while it prohibits those of the workmen... In all... disputes the masters can hold out much longer.... Masters are always and everywhere in a sort of tacit, but constant and uniform combination, not to raise the wages of labour above their actual rate. To violate this combination is everywhere a most unpopular action, and a sort of reproach to a master among his neighbours and equals. [20]

Since competition prevailed in product markets, the diminution in money costs was followed by a diminution in prices. Firms were taking price as a datum; they did not and could not see the behaviour of total effective demand for each product, except in its effects on prices. This is still what happens today under competitive conditions; but in those days such conditions prevailed throughout the economy.

In such conditions, assuming a certain number of innovating firms which introduce new methods of production in order to reduce their costs, the main stimulus to the spread of the new methods is precisely the tendency of prices to fall. Under modern conditions, industrial firms in oligopolistic markets are not compelled to take price as a datum, but can and do influence it, by administering supply with a view to obtaining a given margin over cost (or a given rate of return), not year by year, but over a number of years. In such conditions, assuming again a certain number of innovating firms, the main stimulus to the spread of the new methods no longer originates in the tendency of prices to fall, but in that of wages to rise. What happens is that firms which succeed in raising productivity more rapidly than others do not oppose too strongly the trade unions' claims for higher wages; they may even take the initiative of raising wages in order to attract new workers, and/or to avoid the margin over costs increasing too much, which would provoke an invasion of the market by other firms. Nowadays trade unions are strong and able to generalise and even to speed up wage increases. To a large extent, the very growth of the unions is a result of the same process which has increased the market power of firms in a large section of the economy.

12 *Growth, effective demand and inflation*

The central fact is that in modern conditions many firms are in a position to administer supply in response to variations of demand. This fact has far-reaching consequences both in the short and in the long run.

In the short run, a fall in demand, however caused, is accompanied *not* by a fall in industrial prices (except when cost falls, and then only to a limited extent), but by a corresponding contraction of output. In other words, in the short run, industrial prices have become flexible with respect to cost, and rigid, or very rigid, with respect to demand.

In the long run, effective demand becomes the main determinant of the growth of output and employment. I tried to demonstrate elsewhere that the system of private firms is less and less apt to generate an increase of demand in an endogenous way; but such an increase, owing to the growth of population and to the rise in productivity, is necessary to keep the rate of unemployment relatively low. If this is so, then the growth of demand must originate from stimuli which are external to a given private enterprise system. The outside stimuli in question can be of two kinds: public spending and foreign demand. In the postwar period in the United States, the expansionary inpulse came chiefly from public expenditure, which grew, in its turn, mainly owing to the increase in military spending. In an economy where exports account for no more than 4 per cent of the gross national product, there was, and is, obviously not much to expect from foreign demand. Quite the opposite happened in Japan and in certain countries of Western Europe, such as Italy, the Federal Republic of Germany and France, where foreign demand played a predominant part in stimulating economic growth at a rate which in some countries (Italy, West Germany and Japan) has been nothing short of spectacular.

The expansion of foreign demand owed most to three major factors. The first was the process of establishing the European Economic Community (such an enlargement of the economic space can provide a stimulus to expansion in an oligopolistic industrial structure). The second factor was that developing countries and the socialist countries greatly stepped up their demand on the world market, especially in the last decade. In both cases the sole, or at any rate the chief, impulse comes from public decision-making centres. The third and most important factor was the expansion of the American economy; there is no doubt that, without this, the international trade of the Western world and Japan would not have grown as fast as it has.

If this view is correct, then one of the main factors of growth in the economies of the said countries in the postwar years has been the expansion of the US economy, which, in its turn — it is a sad reflection to make — derived its main stimulus from an increase in military spending. [21] On the other hand, such spending and, more generally, public expenditure is not and cannot be increased in the course of time precisely to the extent needed to keep the economic machine going at the desired speed. Since the forces and interests pushing for expansion of public expenditure follow no strict economic logic, and since, in military spending, a strategic

design is involved, public spending is likely to expand either too slowly or
– much more often – too rapidly. Clearly this is the case now.

The combined effect of too steep an increase in public expenditure for
too long is that the growing competitiveness of European and Japanese
industry, compared with American industry, has been creating mounting
difficulties for the US economy, not to speak of the disruption of the –
admittedly precarious – international monetary equilibrium sustained in
the past by the chronic, but only moderately increasing, deficit in the US
balance of payments,

III   Some empirical findings

So much for theoretical propositions. I will now present, with very brief
comments, some empirical findings [22] which are consistent with (again I
carefully do not say that they 'prove') some of these propositions. In most
cases I shall consider both the Italian and the US economy; the periods
covered are not always the same, because the calculations were made at
different times. The sources of the data are shown in the Appendix to this
chapter.

13   *Agricultural prices: short-run variations* (see section 1 above)

(a)   Italy, 1951–1966 (the t statistic is shown in brackets)

$$P_{a(s)} = 103 \cdot 826 - 0 \cdot 344\, S + 0 \cdot 625\, C_v$$
$$\phantom{P_{a(s)} = } (5 \cdot 825)\ (2 \cdot 748) \qquad (5 \cdot 732)$$

$$R^2 = 0 \cdot 919 \qquad\qquad DW = 1 \cdot 303$$

where $P_{a(s)}$ = wholesale agricultural prices
S = disposable supply of agricultural products (home production + net imports)
C_v = personal consumption at current prices.

(b)   USA, 1948–1968

$$P_{a(s)} = 243 \cdot 411 - 1 \cdot 700\, S_h + 0 \cdot 275\, C_v$$
$$\phantom{P_{a(s)} = } (6 \cdot 965)\ (3 \cdot 628) \qquad (2 \cdot 377)$$

$$R^2 = 0 \cdot 550 \qquad\qquad DW = 1 \cdot 970$$

where S_h = home production.

The equation for Italy is good enough, less so the equation for the United States. Apart, however, from the problems arising from the use of data as aggregated as those in this and in most other equations, note that S_h is only home production; neither net imports nor changes in stocks are taken into account. In any case, the results are consistent with expectations.

14 *Agricultural prices: long-run variations* (see section 1 above)

We calculated a three-year moving average of total average costs and of wholesale prices, and then compared the two curves graphically.

Total average costs were estimated using the formula

$$AC = \alpha \frac{W_a}{\pi_a} + \beta M_a$$

where a and β are the weights of the two basic components of total cost (cost of labour and cost of the goods bought by farmers); we neglected fixed cost and, for simplicity, we took the arbitrary decision of giving fixed weights to the two cost components ($\frac{1}{2}$ and $\frac{1}{2}$).

The results of the comparison were negative for Italy, positive for the United States. In Italy it seems that, in the period 1951–68, costs rose at an average annual rate considerably less than prices: 0·5 and 1·6 respectively. The result has very little meaning, however, because the large increase in productivity (output per man), which statistically contributed to a low rise of average cost, is, in part, illusory. In Italy, in the last fifteen years, large numbers of workers left agriculture. To some extent this meant a genuine increase in productivity, since the reduction in the number of underemployed persons made room for a reorganisation of many farms on more modern standards. But this outflow of manpower also entailed the abandonment of large tracts of land, particularly those which were cultivated only for the farmers' own consumption; the related increase in 'productivity' is only apparent. Figure 2.1 shows that the index of costs ends up at a lower level than that of prices. This means that, if we reduce the trend of productivity, the two curves would practically coincide (this would happen if the average increase in productivity were reduced from the average annual rate of about 7 per cent to one of about 4 per cent).

In the United States the increase in productivity is largely genuine, since emigration from rural areas, and especially emigration implying abandonment of lands, is nowadays relatively limited. The trend in average total cost is therefore not misleading. In the United States, the trend

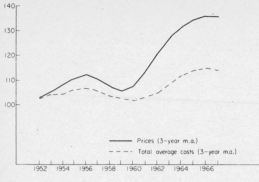

Fig. 2.1   Costs and prices in agriculture, Italy 1951–1968

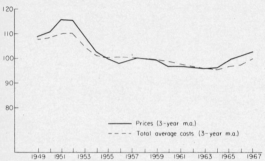

Fig. 2.2   Costs and prices in agriculture, USA 1951–1968

of costs practically coincides with the trend of prices, as appears from Figure 2.2.

15   *Industrial prices; short-run variations* (see section 2 above)

(a)   Italy, 1951–1968

Index numbers:

$$P_{i(s)} = 38\cdot806 + 0\cdot235\ W_i - 0\cdot412\ \pi_i + 0\cdot575\ M_i$$
$$\quad (3\cdot103)\ (6\cdot856) \qquad (5\cdot164) \qquad (4\cdot807)$$

$$R^2\ = 0\cdot928 \qquad\qquad DW\ = 1\cdot354$$

where the difference $W_i - \pi_i$ has been used as a linear approximation of the ratio $W_i/\pi_i = L_i$.

Rates of change (1951–1965):

$$\dot{P}_{i(s)} = 0\cdot084 + 0\cdot400\ \dot{L}_i + 0\cdot386\ \dot{M}_i$$
$$\quad\ (0\cdot521)\ (3\cdot852) \qquad (4\cdot240)$$

$$R^2\ = 0\cdot758 \qquad\qquad DW\ = 1\cdot897$$

(b) USA, 1948–1968

Index numbers:

$$P_{i(s)} = 58\cdot991 + 0\cdot777\ W_i - 0\cdot512\ \pi_i + 0\cdot138\ M_i$$
$$\phantom{P_{i(s)} = 58\cdot991}(7\cdot130)\ (7\cdot877)\qquad (4\cdot276)\qquad (1\cdot973)$$

$$R^2\ =\ 0\cdot959 \qquad\qquad DW\ =\ 1\cdot018$$

Rates of change (1948–1968):

$$\dot{P}_{i(s)} = 1\cdot223 + 0\cdot276\ \dot{L}_i + 0\cdot315\ \dot{M}_i$$
$$\phantom{\dot{P}_{i(s)} = }(3\cdot000)\ (2\cdot017)\qquad (5\cdot178)$$

$$R^2\ =\ 0\cdot665 \qquad\qquad DW\ =\ 2\cdot491$$

$$\dot{P}_{f(s)} = 0\cdot896 + 0\cdot393\ \dot{L}_i + 0\cdot318\ \dot{M}_i$$
$$\phantom{\dot{P}_{f(s)} = }(4\cdot609)\ (6\cdot023)\quad (10\cdot976)$$

$$R^2\ =\ 0\cdot911 \qquad\qquad DW\ =\ 3\cdot191$$

(The first and second equations for the United States refer to 'wholesale industrial prices', the third refers to 'wholesale prices of finished goods'.)

On a first approximation, all these equations give fairly good results. At the aggregate level, one would need to include among the explanatory variables one that in some way represents an index of demand pressure, [23] and it would be advisable to distinguish at least three categories of industries (food, non-durables except food, durables). In any case, it seems that our findings are consistent with the propositions put forth in part I; in particular, the sum of coefficients in the equations using rates of change (= price elasticity with respect to direct cost) is clearly less than unity in both countries (0·786 for Italy, 0·591 or 0·711 for the United States) (see section 2 above).

16 *Industrial prices: long-run variations* (see section 2 above).

Applying the same method that we used for agriculture, we calculated a three-year moving average of total average cost and of prices, and compared the two curves graphically. For the cost calculation, both for Italy and the United States, we gave different (fixed) weights to the cost components (cost of labour and cost of raw materials external to manufacturing industry): 0·50 and 0·50, 0·80 and 0·20, 1·00 and zero. We found that in both countries the variations of prices tend to correspond to the variations of cost, when considering only the cost of labour (see Figs. 2.3 and 2.4).

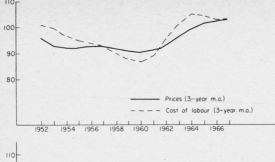

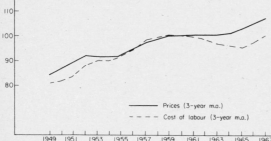

Fig. 2.3　Costs and prices in manufacturing, Italy 1951–196(

Fig. 2.4　Costs and prices in manufacturing, USA 1951–19(

One would expect a higher weight of labour cost in the long run than in the short run, since the long-run cost of home-produced raw materials fully reflects changes in the cost of labour. The correspondence that we found between prices and the cost of labour alone implies that imported raw materials, at least in the two countries and during the periods considered, did not have any significant effects on the trend of costs.

If it is true that in·the long run industrial prices (P_i) tend to coincide with the cost of labour (W_i/π_i), then it is also true that average value productivity ($\pi_i P_i$, i.e. the index number of output per man-hour multiplied by the index number of wholesale industrial prices) tends to equal money wages. This should not be interpreted as a one-way causal relation, since, if we may assume that in the long run the rates of change in both productivity and prices affect wages, we have to assume also that wage changes affect productivity and prices.

17　*Short-run variations in wages (manufacturing)* (sections 5–6 above)

(a)　Italy, 1951–1968

Rates of change:

$$\dot{W}_i = -0.863 + 16.728\,U^{-1} + 1.335\,\dot{V}$$
$$(0.855)\quad(3.056)\qquad(6.463)$$

$$R^2 = 0.860 \qquad\qquad DW = 2.285$$

I then introduced, as an additional explanatory variable, the rates of change in output per man-hour; this proved significant at the 90 per cent level, but the increase in R^2 was very modest.

Further, I introduced in the above equation the number of working hours lost through strikes as an index of trade union 'pushfulness'. R^2 increased considerably, but the coefficient U^{-1} decreased and the t statistic of this coefficient ceased to be significant. This clearly showed a correlation between the hours lost through strikes and unemployment; the reason is easy to understand, since strikes will be less frequent when unemployment is relatively high. After calculating the regression between hours lost and unemployment, I took the deviations between calculated and actual hours lost as the additional explanatory variable for the wage equation. The idea is as follows: if the number and duration of strikes were mechanically related to the degree of unemployment, with no room left for trade union discretionary power, then there would be no need to include such a variable in addition to unemployment and the cost of living, and the correlation coefficient between hours lost and unemployment would be equal to unity. But this is not so, mainly because there is no such mechanical relation and trade unions do have discretionary power. Since we are interested in a measure of this power, we can take the deviations between calculated and actual values in the correlation between the two variables. The substitution of this new variable for the original data of hours lost leaves the multiple correlation coefficient unchanged, but the coefficient of U^{-1} rises and the t statistic again becomes very significant. There was a final difficulty to overcome concerning the timing of the new wage contracts. For instance, in Italy, major strikes took place in 1966, but the new contracts in connection with which the workers struck, became operative only in 1967. We therefore assigned to 1966 the 'normal' deviation (i.e. zero) and carried over to 1967 the 1966 deviation.

The simple correlation between hours lost through strikes (HL) and the inverse of unemployment is

$$HL = 4{\cdot}139 + 202{\cdot}385\ U^{-1}$$
$$(0{\cdot}334)\quad (3{\cdot}168)$$

$$R^2 = 0{\cdot}6210 \qquad DW = 2{\cdot}801$$

Introducing the deviations between calculated and actual values of hours lost, the wage equation becomes

$$\dot{W}_i = -0{\cdot}779 + 14{\cdot}412\ U^{-1} + 1{\cdot}441\ \dot{V} + 0{\cdot}051\ HLD$$
$$\phantom{\dot{W}_i = }(1{\cdot}146)\quad (3{\cdot}864)\quad (10{\cdot}189)\quad (4{\cdot}222)$$

$$R^2 = 0{\cdot}941 \qquad DW = 2{\cdot}426$$

where *HLD* are the said deviations.

(b) USA, 1948–1968

$$\dot{W}_i = 0\cdot180 + 15\cdot147\ U^{-1} + 0\cdot330\ \dot{V}$$
$$\quad\quad (0\cdot255)\quad (4\cdot512)\quad\quad (3\cdot188)$$

$$R^2 = 0\cdot746 \quad\quad\quad DW = 1\cdot305$$

$$\dot{W}_i = 0\cdot238 + 14\cdot544\ U^{-1} + 0\cdot311\ \dot{V} + 0\cdot022\ WSD$$
$$\quad\quad (0\cdot361)\quad (4\cdot614)\quad\quad (3\cdot739)\quad (1\cdot866)$$

$$R^2 = 0\cdot806 \quad\quad\quad DW = 1\cdot385$$

where *WSD* indicates the deviations from the regression relating days lost in work stoppages owing to strikes and lockouts and the inverse of unemployment.

The results for the US, although consistent with the expectations, are less satisfactory than those for Italy. In particular, the inclusion of the *WSD* variable causes less improvement in the statistical fit and that variable is significant only at the 90 per cent level. In the case of the US, however, the number of man-days lost through work stoppages includes not only strikes but also lockouts; moreover, for lack of information, we were unable to take into account, as we did for Italy, the time-lag which sometimes intervenes between national strikes for new contracts and the period in which these contracts become operative. All things considered, then, the results for the United States also support the thesis previously worked out.[24]

An attempt to apply an equation of the kind illustrated above to explain the behaviour of wages in Great Britain also gave positive results, with the difference, compared with Italy and the United States, that there is no correlation between days lost through strikes and the rate of unemployment, so that the latter variable can directly express trade union pressure.[25]

18   *Long-run variations in wages* (see section 8 above)

We proposed to see

(1)   whether empirical indications can be found in support of the hypothesis thar the most dynamic industries are apt to grant the highest wage increases, thus pushing up, via a sort of demonstration effect, all the other wages;

(2)   whether an above-normal increase in wages does affect, after an appropriate delay, the average productivity of the industrial sector;
(3)   whether such an increase in wages does affect, again after an appropriate delay, the rate of increase in industrial employment.

As for the first proposition, I simply refer to the results presented in Chapter 1, section 17, concerning the relations between output per man-hour, hourly earnings and the degree of concentration for fourteen broad categories of Italian industries during the period 1953–64. The values of the Spearman rank correlation coefficients are as follows:

Output per man-hour and degree of concentration   0·76
Earnings and degree of concentration   0·78
Earnings, output per man-hour and degree of concentration   0·72

Similarly, others have obtained positive results for the United States, using different criteria to test the same kind of relations (e.g. J. W. Garbarino, A. M. Ross and W. Goldner, O. Eckstein and T. A. Wilson). [26]
The second proposition (wage increases and productivity) we tested only for Italy and the results were uncertain. We found a positive correlation between three-year moving averages of both wage increases and the rate of increase in physical productivity, after assigning a lag of one period to the first variable; but the correlation coefficient obtained was relatively low (0·30).
The test of the third proposition (wage increases and employment) gave better results. A relatively good (inverse) correlation was found between the rate of employment in industry (workers and employees) and the rate of increase in wages three years earlier; the correlation notably improved after introducing as an additional explanatory variable the rate of change of current investment in industry (at current prices).

$$\dot{O}_i = 4\cdot5568 - 0\cdot4139\ \dot{W}_{\tau-3}$$
$$(6\cdot2369)\ (4\cdot7286)$$

$$R^2 = 0\cdot6507 \qquad DW = 1\cdot8520$$

$$\dot{O}_i = 3\cdot0525 - 0\cdot3036\ W_{\tau-3} + 0\cdot0883\ \dot{I}_i$$
$$(4\cdot6609)\ (4\cdot4524) \qquad (3\cdot6750)$$

$$R^2 = 0\cdot8432 \qquad DW = 2\cdot3761$$

We cannot exclude the possibility that the statistical results are good only because of the peculiarities of the period considered. *In abstracto*, there is little doubt that wage increases tend to influence employment in the opposite direction, owing to the stimulus to labour-saving types of investment; but, the influence at work being very complex, it is possible that that relation asserts itself only when exceptionally high wage increases occur. This did in fact happen in Italy in 1962–63; as a consequence, in the following years, a process of accelerated rationalisation of the industrial structure took place.

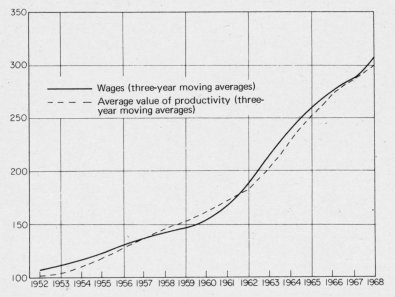

Fig. 2.5   Wages and productivity in manufacturing, Italy 1951–1968

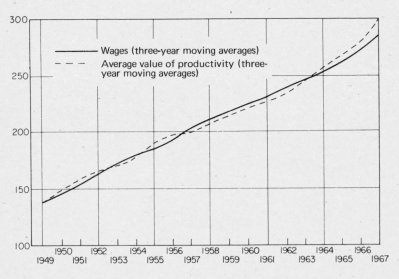

Fig. 2.6   Wages and productivity in manufacturing, USA 1951–1968

94

Granting that, at least for Italy, the above equations express a systematic phenomenon, the implications for economic policy need to be considered. [27]

One final observation. While the correlation between long-run variations in wages and productivity is low when productivity is considered in physical terms, it becomes very high when wages are compared with *value* productivity. Amd if it is true that an interpretation in simple causal terms is misleading, it is also true that this correlation provides a starting point in analysing long-run variations (see Figures 2.5 and 2.6).

This, however, is only an approximation, since the relation between wages and value productivity is based on the price equation for industry, which is valid both in the short and in the long run (the coefficients are different):

$$P_i = a + b \frac{W_i}{\pi_i} + cM_i$$

from which we have

$$W_i = \frac{\pi_i (P_i - a - cM_i)}{b}$$

(Such a formula shows that money wages and raw material prices tend to move in opposite directions).

19 *A few data on prices and productivity*

In section 8 above, I stated that there are reasons to believe that, during an inflationary process, productivity increases, instead of being promoted, are even discouraged. The figures for Italy and the United States given in Table 2.1 seem to support such a proposition.

I refer to wholesale prices and productivity in manufacturing industry, and I consider that an overall inflationary process is under way when industrial prices are rising, since, as we know, in our time the consumer price index keeps going up almost uninterruptedly (though at varying velocities).

In Italy, where so far an inflationary process in the above sense has occurred only twice, in 1962–64 and in 1969, the relation between price and productivity increases is not very clear, although there are indications consistent with our expectation. The indications are much clearer in the case of the United States; during the periods of inflationary pressure (1, 3, 5) productivity increases are considerably lower than in periods of price stablity (2,4). In particular, note that the relatively low average produc-

Table 2.1

| | | Average yearly rates of change | |
		Prices	Productivity
	Italy		
1	1951–1962	−0·8	7·5
2	1962–1964	4·5	6·0
3	1964–1968	1·0	6·8
4	1968–1969	3·4	4·8
	USA		
1	1950–1951	9·5	2·2
2	1951–1955	−0·3	2·9
3	1955–1958	2·9	0·3 (0·5)
4	1958–1964	0·2	4·1
5	1964–1969	2·5	1·8 (1·9)
Yearly averages, periods 1, 3, 5		3·4	1·3
Yearly averages, periods 2, 4		0·0	3·6

tivity increases during the second and third period of rising prices (1955–58 and 1964–69) are to some extent affected by two particular years: 1958, a year of 'recession with inflation', and 1969, a year of very slow industrial growth (we might speak of 'creeping recession with inflation'). In those years productivity did not increase at all; and it is well known that productivity rises tend to slow down during recessions. Even if we exclude those two years, the picture does not change (in the above table corrected averages are shown between parentheses). Moreover, as we have seen, prices continue to rise for some time even when demand for products and demand for labour both slacken, because of the lagged effects of cost increases, so that, in modern conditions, a 'recession with inflation' seems to have become a characteristic feature of a certain stage of the inflationary process. From this standpoint, there is no need to correct the above-mentioned averages.

Finally, we have seen that − contrary to what happened in the past − as a rule rising prices do not mean rising profits; they are often associated with a fall in the rate of profit. In Italy, during the periods of rising prices (1962–64 and 1968–69), there was a fall in the average rate of profit in manufacturing industry. In the United States this rate fell in 1951 and from 1955 to 1958; during the third period of inflationary pressure (1964—69), the average rate of profit fell in two years out of five, in 1967 and in 1969. It must be remembered, however, that the inflationary process which is still under way gathered momentum precisely in 1969.

IV International influences on prices and wages

In any given country, prices and wages are subject not only to domestic, but also to outside influences. Some of the latter have been mentioned here and there, but it will be well to look at them all together, plus some others.

20 *Influences on the determinants of industrial wages*

The following discussion refers to Italy and, for the sake of brevity, I shall limit myself to considering the variables which bring about changes in industrial wages. In each case, I shall indicate to what domestic and international influences these variables, in their turn, are subject. The variables, it will be recalled, are three in number: the cost of living (V), the rate of unemployment (U) and trade union pressure (TUP), the latter quantified by the number of man-hours lost through strikes (or more precisely, by considering the deviations between calculated and actual values in the simple correlation between hours lost and the degree of unemployment). Some of the domestic and international factors which influence these three variables have already been discussed either in this or the previous chapter: P_a and P_{ae} — domestic and European agricultural wholesale prices; P_i — industrial wholesale prices; M_i — prices of imported raw materials; P_{iwo} — international wholesale prices of manufactures; P_r — retail prices of goods; A — index of rents; W_r/π_r — labour costs, i.e. the ratio of wages to 'efficiency', in retail trade; I — industrial investment; UN — degree of unused capacity; E — exports. Other factors are not examined in this book (SE — price index for services; EM — emigration; DLE — demand for labour in the principal continental European countries). In Figures 2.7—2.9 the symbols for variables wholly or largely influenced by international factors are underlined.

The cost of living is indirectly influenced, via the wholesale prices of manufactures, by the prices of imported raw materials and the international wholesale prices of manufactures; another indirect influence on the cost of living comes from domestic agricultural prices, which, at least part, depend on international agricultural prices and on the European

97

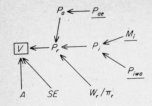

Fig. 2.7   Cost of living

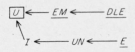

Fig. 2.8   Unemployment

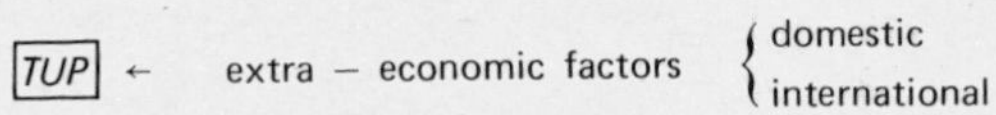

$$\boxed{TUP} \leftarrow \quad \text{extra} - \text{economic factors} \quad \begin{cases} \text{domestic} \\ \text{international} \end{cases}$$

Fig. 2.9 Trade union pressure

Economic Community's common agricultural policy.

Unemployment is affected by emigration, which in turn depends on demand for labour in the principal European countries (and also, to a very slight extent, on labour demand in industrial countries overseas); it is also influenced by exports, via the degree of unused capacity and industrial investment.[28]

Finally, trade union pressure depends to some extent on the current cost of living and expected changes therein, and this is accounted for, at least statistically, in the variable V; it is likewise influenced by the degree of unemployment, which, to avoid duplication, is statistically eliminated by the method explained earlier in this chapter (section 17 above). But in addition to these economic factors, trade union pressure is influenced also by extra-economic ones, of both domestic and international origin. Among the former are, for example, the quality of leadership, union strategy and its links with action by political parties. International influences include the demonstration effect emanating from the policy of central trade union organisations in other industrial countries. This takes the analysis right into the field of political history, where knowledge of actual facts needs to be combined with qualitative interpretation. To take an example: surely, Italy's 'hot autumn' in 1969 in many ways reflected the French 'May crisis' of 1968. In France, trade union leaders were largely taken by surprise when the factions of the extreme left went into action. Italian trade unions tried to take advantage of the French experience. They chose a propitious moment, when several major collective agreements, including that of the metal and engineering workers, came up for renewal in the autumn of 1969, and in good time put forward a number of highly ambitious claims. The intention was, first, to meet the workers' expectations whetted by the results achieved by their mates in France, and secondly, to avoid being outflanked from the left by extra-parliamentary groups. At a certain point the employers gave in without unduly strong resistance, not least because they wanted to uphold union influence — unions clearly being regarded as the lesser evil in comparison with the extra-parliamentary groups of the extreme left.

This is only one example of the way in which union action can be influenced and stimulated by a demonstration effect emanating from abroad. Certainly, some concomitance in the fluctuations of union militancy in different countries can be detected in their annual statistics of days lost through strikes. Of course, the intensity of trade union pressure varies greatly from one country to another, and there is no simple synchronism. Yet the degree of concomitance is striking enough. 'Hot' years in different countries often coincide, e.g. 1953 and 1954, 1961, 1962 and 1963 and, it would seem, 1970. [29]

The upward pressure on Italian wages originating abroad, and especially in European countries, work not only in the short, but also in the long run. They are propagated mainly through the flows of migrant labour. There can be no doubt that the faster pace of wage rises in Italy during the sixties owed at least something to a tendency for absolute wage levels to even out internationally (at given exchange rates); in any event this applies to the wages paid by medium-sized and large firms. [30]

21 *The relative strength of domestic and international inflationary pressures*

On the basis of the above analysis, responsibility for inflationary pressure in Italy during the last five years can be imputed as follows.

1   In 1969, until the hot autumn, prices were pushed up chiefly and directly by international factors, to wit, a rise of some 8 per cent in the prices of imported raw materials and of about 4 per cent in the international prices of manufactures.

2   During and immediately after the hot autumn certain products were in short supply and their prices experienced an additional upward thrust.

3   During 1970 external pressure via raw materials fell off sharply, but the remarkable rise in the international prices of finished goods contributed to raising their domestic prices too, via an upward shift of the limit to

price increases; at the same time the upward push of labour costs became much stronger, at any rate on industrial wholesale prices and on the retail prices of goods and services.

4 The upward push of labour costs continued in 1971, but at a lower rate.

5 In 1972 and, even more, in 1973 the external upward pressure on domestic prices via raw materials and manufactures became the dominating factor of the inflationary process.

An analytical examination of the inflationary process in Italy in recent years will be presented in Chapter 4, section 11.

Notes

[1] David Ricardo, *On the Principles of Political Economy, and Taxation*, Chapter XXX.

[2] In Europe the prices of agricultural products are interrelated, not only because of the agreements on minimum levels in the Common Market, but also for other reasons. Therefore, it would probably be advisable to include, among the explanatory variables in the short-run price equation, also a weighted average of European prices for agricultural products.

[3] The coefficient γ is to be conceived as the product of the relative weight (γ') of the cost of labour over direct cost and an index of variation of this relative weight; this index (γ'') is equal to unity when the relative change in the cost of labour is entirely shifted onto price, and less than unity when such a shift is only partial. A similar distinction applies to $\delta = \delta' \times \delta''$. The sum $\gamma' + \delta' = 1$ by definition, since total direct cost is the reference cost – each of the two indices of variation, γ'' and δ'', is equal to or less than unity, so that $\gamma + \delta \leqslant 1$. The argument worked out in the text is that $\gamma + \delta < 1$ in the short run and $\gamma + \delta = 1$ in the long run.

[4] For instance, General Motors administer the prices of their products in view of the 'highest attainable rate of return on capital', and this 'is a long-run objective: the company does not necessarily try to maximize its return in any given year, but rather over a period of years, which may be characterized by wide fluctuations of output' (United States Senate Committee on the Judiciary, Sub-Committee on Anti-Trust and Monopoly, *Administered Prices: Automobiles,* p. 106). Other large firms tend to follow a target mark-up criterion of pricing, which, as we have seen (Chapter 1, section 4), can be considered as practically equivalent to the target-return criterion. Such criteria seem to be used in mature and well-

established industries, which, year by year, produce the bulk of industrial commodities. Firms operating in new industries follow different criteria, as Dirlam, Kaplan and Lanzilotti have shown (*Pricing in Big Business, A Case Approach,* The Brookings Institution, Washington, 1958, Chapter 2). However, these other methods either do not significantly depart from the methods of target mark-up and target-return pricing, or consist simply in 'following the leader'.

[5] It seems that during 1969 the price of the main steel products was put up because of the high pressure of demand, which occurred simultaneously with a lack of unused capacity in virtually all industrial countries.

[6] By wages I mean hourly money earnings of production workers.

[7] This is the reason why I cannot accept the thesis worked out by Edwin Kuh in his article 'A Productivity Theory of Wage Levels — An Alternative to the Phillips Curve' *Review of Economic Studies* 34, October 1967, pp. 333—61. In fact, Professor Kuh is using an equation similar to (2.3b) to explain short-run variations in wages.

[8] Karl Marx, *Das Kapital* vol. I, Chapter XXV.

[9] At the time of the classical economists and of Marx, when trade unions either did not exist or were very weak, the cost of living played a role not in the short but in the long run (over a number of years); this was emphasised by all classical economists.

[10] Eckstein and Wilson, in a study on the determinants of money wages in American industry, distinguish between 'key industries' (a group of heavy industries with a high degree both of concentration and of unionisation) and the other industries, and find evidence both that the industries of the first group act as wage leaders and that their profits, alongside unemployment, are a significant explanatory variable (profits in their turn are influenced by variations in productivity). Pierson distinguishes between industries with a high and industries with a low degree of unionisation and finds that profits represent one of the explanatory variables of the wage equation for the second group of industries. See O. Eckstein and T. A. Wilson, 'The Determination of Money Wages in American Industry' *Quarterly Journal of Economics* 76, August 1962, pp. 379—414; G. Pierson, 'The Effect of Union Strength on the US Phillips Curve' *American Economic Review* 58, June 1968, pp. 456—67.

[11] A different matter is productivity *per man*, which, owing to the tendency of firms to reduce the number of hours worked rather than the number of workers employed in periods of recession, obviously tends to move in strict correspondence to the movements of output; the correspondence is not so close, but still considerable, if one compares the

changes of productivity per man-hour with the degree of unemployment, so that is does not seem correct to include unemployment *and* productivity per man among the explanatory variables.

[12] That the cost of living has become a relevant explanatory variable for short-run wage changes because of trade union pressure is indicated not only by analysing the results of the articles by Phillips and Lipsey, which cover a long span of economic history, but also by certain empirical findings, showing that in our time the variations in the cost of living have a more direct and larger explanatory value in the industries where the degree of unionisation is high than in industries where it is low. Cf. Pierson, 'Union strength', op.cit.

[13] Cf. United Nations, *Incomes in Postwar Europe. A study of Policies, Growth and Distribution*, part II of *Economic Survey of Europe in 1965*, Geneva 1967, Chapter 3, p. 16.

[14] Although the income of the self-employed in agriculture formally includes not only 'remuneration' of their labour but also an element of profit and one of farm rent, it is often in the end effect lower than the income of wage earners in the modern sector. This circumstance adds impetus to the flight from the land, and, taking the system as a whole, the mere fact that the number of self-employed workers is declining tends, other things being equal, to raise the distributive share of wage earners.

[15] On the effects of union action on the distribution of income, see Michael Kalecki, 'Class Struggle and the Distribution of Income', published in *Kyklos* (1, 1971) after the author's death.

[16] In Italy, during the last ten years, the distributive share of dependent labour increased appreciably to the detriment not only of the self-employed workers' share (which diminished mainly because their number declined) but also of profits.

[17] See L. Spaventa, 'Effetti distributivi del processo inflazionistico in Italia nel decennio 1953–1962' *Moneta e credito*, December 1963.

[18] Since the inverse of the unemployment rate can be and has been considered as an index of excess demand for labour, some economists speak of demand-pull inflation even when inflation is due to wage increases. This argument obscures the question, because demand for labour and demand for goods are conceptually different. Besides, as we have seen, the unemployment rate is nowadays by no means the only factor influencing wage changes.

[19] In developing countries, where government tries to promote a development process by investment in public works and in industry, inflation is generated mainly by demand, because agricultural products account for a

relatively high proportion of national income and their supply, in those countries, is very rigid.

[20] Adam Smith, *The Wealth of Nations*, Book 1, Chapter VIII.

[21] Many economists, not only in the United States but also elsewhere, hope that the American political leaders will be able to reduce military expenditure, and gradually and continuously increase at a much higher rate than at present expenditure for civilian development as well as expenditure to promote the development of backward countries. While such aspirations are much to be approved, we should not hide from ourselves the serious obstacles which make such a shift very difficult. One obstacle arises from the fact that industries working for the Defense Department are, as a rule, different from those working for civilian public investment, and this makes the 'conversion problem' a very difficult one. Another, even more important obstacle closely connected with the first, is that formidable complex of interests — involving not only the military establishment and a good number of big corporations, but also relatively large groups of workers — which the late President Eisenhower dubbed 'the military-industrial complex' and which has become very influential in shaping American policy in general.

[22] My thanks are due to Carlo Del Monte and Maurizio Piperno, who collected the data, made the calculations and offered advice in working out the empirical tests.

[23] In the short run, at least in an open economy like Italy's, the price elasticity with respect to direct cost is less than unity, owing mainly to the pressure of foreign competition (see section 2 above). To test this second proposition, we recalculated, for Italy, a variant of the industrial price equation in terms of rates of change, including also the index of the international prices of manufactured goods (P_{iwo}). This is the result:

$$\dot{P}_i = -0 \cdot 066 + 0 \cdot 299\, \dot{L}_i + 0 \cdot 388\, M_i + 0 \cdot 463\, \dot{P}_{iwo}$$
$$t = (0 \cdot 212)\,(4 \cdot 253)\quad (5 \cdot 011)\quad (2 \cdot 964)$$

$$R^2 = 0 \cdot 808 \qquad DW = 1 \cdot 904$$

For comparison, a similar equation was calculated for the United Kingdom, with the following result:

$$\dot{P}_i = 0 \cdot 371\, \dot{L}_i + 0 \cdot 347\, \dot{M}_i + 0 \cdot 272\, \dot{P}_{iwo}$$
$$(1 \cdot 243)\quad (4 \cdot 228)\quad (2 \cdot 060)$$

$$R^2 = 0 \cdot 969 \qquad DW = 1 \cdot 922$$

The data are taken from the *National Institute Economic Review*.

[24] Like others, we found that after 1962 observed values are systematically lower than calculated values, showing that some change did occur since that year. According to Pierson and to Solow, this is likely to be a consequence of the introduction of wage–price guideposts. See Pierson, 'Union strength', op.cit. If the guidepost hypothesis is correct, then a dummy variable has to be introduced after 1962, as was done by Pierson. The equation then becomes

$$\dot{W} = 0{\cdot}481 + 14{\cdot}433\ U^{-1} + 0{\cdot}389\ \dot{V} + 0{\cdot}018\ WSD - 0{\cdot}725\ D$$
$$(0{\cdot}823)\quad (5{\cdot}229)\qquad (4{\cdot}466)\quad (1{\cdot}719)\qquad (2{\cdot}423)$$

$$R^2 = 0{\cdot}861 \qquad DW = 1{\cdot}746$$

The dummy is significant and the fit improves. However, in practice the guideposts lasted until 1966; putting the dummy equal to zero for 1967 and 1968, R^2 falls to $0{\cdot}842$ and the dummy becomes significant only at the 10 per cent level. This result seems to be rather unfavourable to the guidepost hypothesis.

[25] Here is the equation, referring to the period 1952–71:

$$\dot{W} = -0{\cdot}491 + 2{\cdot}479\ U^{-4} + 0{\cdot}849\ \dot{V} + 0{\cdot}250\ DL$$
$$(0{\cdot}812)\ (1{\cdot}768)\qquad (6{\cdot}649)\quad (2{\cdot}666)$$

$$R^2 = 0{\cdot}858 \qquad DW = 2{\cdot}301$$

where W is the index of weekly wage rates in industry, U the percentage of unemployment, V the cost of living as measured by the retail prices of goods and services, and DL the number of days lost through strikes (in millions). All the data are taken from the *National Institute Economic Review*, except those for days lost through strikes, which are from the International Labour Office's *Yearbook of Labour Statistics*.

The U^{-4} variable was considered instead of the usual U^{-1} variable on the basis of a suggestion put forward by Lipsey in his 1960 article, quoted in the bibliography in the Appendix to Chapter 1. The U^{-4} variable is statistically significant (at the 90 per cent level), whereas the U^{-1} variable is not significant, probably because the hypothetical Phillips curve in the period considered has got a greater curvature than in the past. Why the number of days lost through strikes is, in Great Britain, not correlated with unemployment, so that the unions' 'pushfulness' seems to be unaffected by this particular index of tension in the labour market, is a matter for reflection — which I leave to the reader.

[26] *Quarterly Journal of Economics*, May 1950 and August 1962.

[27] I give one instance, with reference to Italy. If one of the targets of economic policy is to increase employment in industry without attempt-

ing to push down the long-run increase in wages, then it becomes necessary to promote the growth and rationalisation of small businesses, since big corporations as a rule are more dynamic with regard to productivity but less dynamic as far as employment is concerned.

[28] See Chapter 1, sections 7 and 12.

[29] The relevant statistics will be found in the International Labour Office's *Yearbook of Labour Statistics*, 1961 and 1969; but they refer only to days lost through *official* strikes, so that the figures are not fully comparable. The countries for which I compared figures were Italy, the United Kingdom, France, Western Germany, the United States and Japan.

[30] On the whole question of international inflationary pressures compare my analysis with that put forward by Gardner Ackley in his recent book *Stemming World Inflation*, Atlantic Institute, Paris 1971 (Chapter IV, 'International inflation: the exporting and importing price level').

Appendix

Sources of data

For Italy:

Agricultural prices, supply of agricultural products, personal consumption, employment in agriculture: *I conti economici nazionali dell'Italia; Supplemento al bollettino mensile di statistica*, no. 1, January 1970; *Rilevazione campionaria delle forze di lavoro*.

Prices, output per man-hour in manufacturing, prices of imported raw materials: *Annuario statistico italiano; Bollettino mensile di statistica; I conti economici nazionali dell'Italia; Statistiche del lavoro; Relazione generale sulla situazione economica del paese*.

International prices of manufactures: United Nations, *Statistical Yearbook, 1969*.

Hourly earnings in manufacturing, unemployment, cost of living, hours lost through strikes: *Statistiche del lavoro; Rilevazione campionaria delle forze di lavoro; Annuario statistico italiano*.

All the Italian publications listed above are published by the Central Statistical Institute, with the exception of Labour Statistics (Ministry of Labour) and the General Report on the Economic Situation of the Country (Ministry of the Budget).

For the United States:

All the data were taken from the Statistical Appendix to the Annual Report of the Council of Economic Advisers, *Economic Report of the President* (February 1969), except those for 'man-days idle for strikes and lockouts', which were culled from various issues of the *US Statistical Yearbook*.

3 Structural Inflation and Incomes Policy

In present conditions, the wholesale prices of industrial products diminish only when money wages rise at lower rate than productivity, assuming that international prices of raw materials and finished products remain stationary; any general decline in these prices in consequence of a fall in demand can be ruled out.

1 Wages and productivity: comparative changes

Can it happen, over a number of years, that wages rise systematically less than productivity?

It can happen, but only when a country has a large pool of unemployed workers and underemployed farm labour, or can draw on a pool of workers and unemployed in neighbouring countries. However, because of diaphragms within the labour market and because of the unions' bargaining power, money wages tend to rise even in the presence of a large reserve of disposable labour; indeed, when the process of accumulation quickens, so does the pace of wage increases and hence tends to catch up with or overtake the rate of increase in productivity.

Even when labour is in ample supply, therefore, the rate of increase in money wages on the average tends to come close to the rate of increase in productivity. It follows that even in that case labour costs either remain stationary or diminish only slightly, so that, in turn, the wholesale prices of industrial products on the average tend either to remain stationary or to fall only very little. But these are exceptional conditions; in the more frequent conditions, these prices tend to rise.

Since the second world war two European countries found themselves for some time with a particularly copious supply of labour. They were Italy, with mass unemployment and considerable underemployment in agriculture, and Western Germany, with large-scale immigration first from East Germany and later from other European countries.

In Italy, unemployment amounted to some 10 per cent of the labour force during the fifties, and as a result industrial wages rose less than productivity, and the wholesale prices of industrial products declined slightly (at an average annual rate 0·7 per cent — see Appendix, Table 3.1). In the sixties and early seventies the situation was strikingly different.

2 Industry and agriculture

In the short period, the question of comparative increases in wages and productivity is relevant only to industry and not to agriculture, where in the short period prices depend not on cost but on demand and supply. In principle, there is no obstacle to even a quite considerable fall in the wholesale prices of agricultural products. In the case of certain products, there is indeed no obstacle. But as regards the principal agricultural commodities, a price decline is impeded by artificial obstacles, in so far as many countries have adopted some sort of support policy for agricultural wholesale prices. In industry, concentration has led to a tendency towards downward price rigidity while wages have not only become rigid downwards, but have tended to rise systematically as a result of the emergence and growing strength of unions, which in turn had a lot to do with the process of concentration; in agriculture, no such process took place or, if it did, it generated no appreciable market power. As a result, agriculture found itself in growing difficulties. Agricultural wages rose along with industrial ones, and the prices of industrial producer goods rose or at any rate did not fail; but in the short period farm prices remain subject to unlimited fluctuations in either direction, up or down.

This is why a number of compensatory measures were adopted, beginning with some sort of price supports, not only for the above-mentioned economic reasons but also for political ones (the weight of the farm vote, problems of social stability).

3 Structural inflation

The end result of all this is that in today's conditions the wholesale prices neither of industrial nor of agricultural products can fall to any considerable extent in the long run. Either they fall only a little, or they remain stationary or, the most frequent case, they tend to rise.

But even at best (constant or slightly declining wholesale prices), the cost of living tends to rise. Consumer prices go up because the rising costs of retail trade (labour costs, shop rents, indirect taxes) are passed on in full to consumers, whereas any decline in prices, especially for agricultural products, is *not* passed on to consumers or only to a minimal extent; the prices of personal services rise (generally by as much as the average wage

108

increase) and so do those of public services (fares); and house rents, which count for much in the cost of living, go up as well.

All this adds up to structural inflationary pressure. It is evident in the cost of living, but derives from wholesale prices, in so far as these, at best, remain roughly constant. Experience has shown this inflationary pressure to afflict all Western countries; it is just a question of degree.

The assumption behind the argument so far was relative stability of international prices for raw materials and industrial products. If world raw material prices rise, cost-push tends to drive up the domestic prices of manufactures. If world prices for manufactures rise, domestic prices tend to go up as well because of an upward shift of the limit beyond which firms which produce goods entering into international trade cannot raise their prices. In both cases domestic consumer prices tend to rise and therefore wages in their turn tend to go up. In such conditions it is most unlikely that money wages will rise less, or no more, than productivity.

It has been said that some degree of inflation, even if small, is an inevitable consequence of an expansion of output. Expressed in these general terms, the argument is wrong. What is true is that some inflationary pressure derives from the structure of modern economies, and that, given this structure, the pace of expansion and of inflation condition each other within certain limits.

In proof of the statement that expanding production need not necessarily generate inflation, it may be worthwhile looking at the nineteenth-century movements of prices and wages in countries which at that time were in full growth, such as Great Britain and the United States. All prices were on a falling trend, while money wages fluctuated in absolute value (and not only with respect to their rate of increase) and real wages were on a rising trend largely attributable to falling prices.[1] Barring years of acute depression, output expanded in both countries even during the long periods of falling prices (1820 to 1842, and 1871 to 1897). During the only period of general and prolonged price falls in the twentieth century (1929 to 1933), by contrast, both output and employment fell sharply, mostly in consequence of the drop in industrial production.[2] During periods of expansion in our century, especially since the end of the second world war, wholesale prices at best remained more or less stationary and consumer prices rose in all countries, but on the whole less where the rate of expansion was highest.[3]

4   *Structural inflation in Italy during the last twenty years*

There is a clear example of structural inflation in the movements of prices in Italy during the fifties, or more precisely, during the years 1952 to 1961 (see Appendix, Table 3.1). During that period wholesale prices remained virtually stationary, but the cost of living rose at an annual average rate of 2·7 per cent. The stability of agricultural and industrial wholesale prices was due, in the first place, to the fact that wages in both sectors rose less than productivity. In industry, wages rose over the whole period by 52 per cent, and productivity by 78 per cent. Given that raw material prices hardly changed and that, for industry as a whole, raw materials account for about one third of direct cost, direct cost in industry declined during the period by about 10 per cent, and the prices of industrial products only by 6 per cent. The discrepancy is attributable mostly to two circumstances. First, a number of industrial products are sheltered from international competition in various ways (e.g. high transport costs), and secondly, industrial prices in the leading industrial countries remained almost stationary throughout the period and thus exerted no downward pressure on Italian prices. Consequently, the gross profit margin per unit of output as well as the distributive share of profits rose in industry, more especially in manyfacturing (see Appendix, Tables 3.1 and 3.2).

Despite the virtual stability of wholesale prices, retail prices rose and so did, even more, the cost of living. What happened?

The price of goods in the shops went up for two main reasons. First, because of higher labour costs in retail trade, and secondly because of higher shop rents. Labour costs, in their turn, climbed because wages (or the rewards imputable to work) rose more than the 'efficiency' of retail trade, which may be measured by the ratio of the volume of consumer goods sold and the number of persons employed. Since wages and rewards for work in retail trade rose over the ten years as a whole at much the same rate as other wages, more especially industrial wages, the increase in the cost of living must be explained largely by the insufficient improvement in retail trade efficiency.

Shop rents rose very sharply, presumably in line with house rents, which would be something like 10 per cent a year or even more, allowing for rent control and its gradual relaxation as well as for free rents. Supposing that shop rents account for 10 per cent of retail trade costs, their rise may, on the average, have pushed the retail price index up by almost one point a year. This argument rests on the assumption that shopkeepers can, even in the short period, pass cost increases on to consumers in full or in large part. Of course many shopkeepers own their own premises, others had and in decreasing measure still have the advantage of paying low, controlled rents, and some pay free rents. It is this last group which is assumed to be transferring onto retail prices any rent increase they have to pay; the other two groups enjoy a differential gain, not as shopkeepers, but as owners of premises or as tenants of rent-controlled ones.

The prices of personal services are pushed up by rising remunerations, those of real services by a rise in public transport fares, which is due jointly to rising remunerations and to low efficiency gains of public transport.

If shop rents do quite a bit to raise retail prices, house rents do much more to push up the cost of living; from 1952 to 1961, they were responsible for roughly one quarter of its total rise. It seems, from a recent survey of the Central Statistical Institute, that about half of all heads of households are house owners. But, as urbanisation proceeds apace, hosts of workers rent houses or rooms in the towns and it avails them little that in their home village their parents live in a house of their own. The Central Statistical Institute's rent index is a weighted average of controlled and uncontrolled rents in very diverse urban centres; in some areas the index overrates the increase, but in others, especially the most industrialised and congested ones, it underrates it. Taking wage earners as a whole, the rent increase is probably understated by the index, and hence the real wage rise somewhat overstated.

During the years 1952 to 1961, then, an 'incomes policy' was harshly enforced by huge unemployment, and money wages rose less than productivity. Nevertheless, prices on the whole did not stay put. Retail prices went up, and so, rather more, did the cost of living. There were a number of reasons for this, but the chief one had to do with building, seeing that not only house rents rose, but shop rents as well. As a result, real wages rose only about one third as much as money wages − 1·4 as against 4 per cent annually.

The reason why it seemed useful to discuss conditions in the fifties at such length is that in those years structural inflation can, as it were, be seen in its purest state; the rate of increase in the cost of living is about as low as it can be. Thereafter, things changed. In the years 1961 to 1970, wholesale prices rose by about 2·6 per cent annually, and the cost of living by some 4·2 per cent at an annual average. The pace of inflation, clearly, was much faster, but the difference between the two rates of increase was not all that much smaller.

5 Prices and wages policy

It would seem, then, that in present conditions it is not possible to keep the cost of living stable. On the other hand it may be *very* difficult, but not absolutely impossible, in a situation of near full employment, to achieve

111

two related aims, namely, to keep wholesale prices more or less stable and to contain the rise in the cost of living within very narrow limits, say 2 or 2·5 per cent annually.

Stability of wholesale prices presupposes that four conditions are met. The first two of them have to do with agricultural prices, the other two with industrial prices. The first condition is that in the short period (from one year to the next) the supply of agricultural products must grow at much the same rate as demand, and this depends on the marginal propensity to consume agricultural products. It may happen that in any one year supply rises less than demand, and then prices will rise. But this does not rule out price stability over the average of a certain number of years, because, when supply exceeds demand, prices may fall. This will not happen if the government supports farm prices, or if in some way (by massive stockpiling or possibly even by the destruction of some commodities) it brings supply down to match demand. Nor will it happen if wholesalers pay such low farmgate prices that it is not worthwhile for the producers to bring in their whole harvest. This means that part of the harvest is destroyed in the fields and as a result wholesale prices can remain constant or even rise, while producer prices decline. The second condition is that in the long run the cost of agricultural production must remain more or less constant, which means (assuming relative stability of industrial prices) that farm wages must, on the average, rise at the same rate as productivity. The third condition is that industrial prices, which rise in sectors of below-average productivity gains, must fall where productivity increases at rates above the average. The fourth condition is that industrial wages must rise at the same rate as average productivity. This happens spontaneously only when the cost of living goes up very slowly and when the supply of labour is fairly large; it cannot happen spontaneously, i.e. without government intervention, when the system approaches full employment.

Finally, there is another condition of stability which concerns both agricultural and industrial wholesale prices, and this is relative stability of international prices for raw materials as well as for finished products.

Supposing, then, that wholesale prices remain reasonably stable, the next question is on what conditions the rise in the cost of living can be kept down to no more than, say, 2 or 2·5 per cent.

First condition: retail trading costs must not rise, or rise only very little. In essence, this implies that indirect taxes must not go up, that the barriers which protect wholesale trade, especially in agricultural products, must be lowered, and that the efficiency of retail trade must grow at a rate very close to that at which the system's average productivity increases, so that labour costs in retail trade rise either not at all or only a little.

Second condition: house rents must rise only moderately.

The first condition can be met if government refrains from raising indirect taxes and successfully promotes a reorganisation of the wholesale trade in agricultural products on a new basis, at the same time making retail trade more efficient. The best thing the authorities can do towards this latter end is probably to encourage the speedy and widespread creation of large commercial units, such as supermarkets and co-operatives, as well as joint purchasing arrangements by small units. However, there are many small shopkeepers and they carry political weight; it would be rash to underestimate the difficulties which government action of this kind is bound to encounter. On the other hand, it is an observed fact that in periods of strong expansion of production and consumption the number of persons employed in trade hardly rises, so that the efficiency of trade — measured by the ratio of the volume of consumer goods sold to the number of persons employed — grows more quickly. At such times government action designed to speed up efficiency gains in trade has its best chances of success, provided the underlying tendency is spontaneously favourable.

The second condition, a limited rise of house rents, can be satisfied by consistent government intervention, not only to hold rent increases down by legal measures, but also, and especially, to encourage an expansion of supply. This can be done by credit incentives, and by stepping up low-cost housing programmes in areas made available for development by appropriate legislation.

Already it must be clear that the conditions for a successful incomes policy are a good deal more complex than most people think.

So far, we have looked only at a few particular prices and costs which enter into the cost of living. Beyond these, is it at all possible, outside credit and monetary policy, to do anything about prices and wages generally? This, after all, is what incomes policy is all about.

Even without any upward pressure emanating from world markets, the difficulties of putting an incomes policy into effect are formidable. Somehow or other means must be found of controlling or regulating, not of course all wages and all prices, which is impossible, but at least wages and prices in strategic sectors, as well as of holding back the increase in trading margins and in rents. As though this were not enough, there are the trade unions to reckon with and their new policy. In the most advanced capitalist countries, including Italy, the unions are increasingly bent on strengthening their bargaining position as regards not only wages, but also such

113

matters as working conditions on the factory floor and, well beyond that, social policy — or what, in some countries, is called reform policy. And so incomes policy is up against social dialectics as such, or, in Marxist terms, the class struggle in the form it has in recent years assumed in the countries of high capitalism. This cannot be hemmed in and, even if it were possible on abstract assumptions, one would not wish it to happen. The lashes which unions mete out to employers in the form of wage rises occasionally well beyond productivity gains, may be salutary to the extent that they lead firms to modernise and to change their production methods. To count working hours lost through strikes as a pure debit item in the social economy reveals a narrow view pardonable in an accountant or book-keeper, but not in an economist. It is true, of course, that if the whip is applied too strongly and too often, more firms go bankrupt and the pace of production slackens, fewer hours are worked and unemployment increases. On the other hand, an accelerated increase in wages tends to speed up the increase in demand for consumer goods, including imported ones, and thus brings about a deterioration in the balance of payments. This in turn sooner or later provokes credit restrictions, with a consequent fall in investment and employment. It is this kind of problems and dangers (rather than necessarily any wish to defend vested interests) which has led many economists to recommend some sort of incomes policy.

But there is no golden rule. It is neither possible nor desirable to stifle the social dialectics by an incomes policy. But this does not mean that one has to resign oneself to a stop—go pattern in which strong growth is followed by near-stagnation or recession, with mounting unemployment. On the contrary, a great deal needs to be done, on the part of public decision centres no less than of the trade unions. And the very first thing to do is to make a critical reappraisal of the forces in play.

On the side of public decision centres, we need a thoroughgoing analysis of the branches of activity which, in each period, assume a leading role in the movement of wages and of prices. Government can play an active part in negotiations for the renewal of labour contracts in these branches, and also influence the pricing policy of public utilities as well as of price leaders among firms in the private and the public sector. The means of exerting pressure are there; all that is needed is to use them judiciously. Active public intervention in the determination both of wages and of prices is particularly important in the case of goods directly or indirectly used as means of production by all firms (in economic theory, these are Sraffa's — and the classics' — 'non-luxury' or 'basic' commodities).

Official action would likewise be helpful in arranging a reasonable time schedule of contract renewals, so as to minimise the risk of several large and widespread wage rises coinciding in any one year. And government can take action in two sectors in which its direct influence is very considerable, namely, in public employment (in the broadest sense) and in construction. One can but hope that the lesson of past errors has been heeded. To take the example of Italy, periods of conspicuous pay increases in public employment (e.g. 1961–63) alternated with years when salaries hardly went up at all (e.g. 1964–69); pay rises simply were not planned, as they could and should have been. During the last two years the unions which represent public employees have adopted the strategy of blue-collar unions and have pressed a number of claims which, while in some cases justified by government negligence, ultimately overshot the mark and became all too reminiscent of corporatism. Yet the government was unable, or unwilling, to resist the unions' claims. In construction, the ruling parties are guilty of two sins of omission: they failed to do anything about a reform of town planning (until only just recently, and then not nearly enough), and they did not do enough to provide more public housing. This left the field open for scandalous housing speculation, allowed rents to soar and prevented residential building from being used as an instrument of countercyclical policy.

Generally speaking, the whole set of measures required for achieving what might be called near-stability of the purchasing power of money is likely to be the more effective the faster productivity rises. In Italy, productivity has, in the past, been observed to rise fastest in the most concentrated industries.[4] This suggests that there is a case for removing the obstacles to industrial concentration, and indeed for actively encouraging it. To do so would, of course, mean allowing some groups to create and strengthen positions of market power, with the consequent possibility of monopolistic practices. But this is not a sufficient reason for impeding the process of concentration, which creates larger production units, speeds up technical and organisational progress, and ultimately preserves and enhances competitive strength on world markets.

To suggest that there is a case for encouraging the process of concentration does not, of course, imply any denial of the vitality and growth potential of small firms. First of all, there are the small 'satellite' firms which are suppliers of goods and services to the big ones, and which prosper and expand with them; there is a good example of this in Piedmont, where Fiat and a few other giant concerns directly or indirectly keep the wheels of industry turning throughout the whole region. Secondly, there exists in every 'industry' — for example, in the 'textile industry' —

a more or less extensive range of products,[5] some of which lend themselves to mass production while others do not. In the case of the first, there is every advantage in encouraging concentration; for the others, qualitative specialisation may be preferable, for which small firms may be more suitable. All in all, however, it does seem that in many industries growth depends on their biggest firms. It is on this basis, and, of course, after critical examination of each industry's structure and development, that the statement about the expediency of promoting industrial concentration can be upheld.

6 Incomes policy and reform policy

So much for the more obvious quantitative aspects of the problem: increases in wages, productivity and prices. But, given that in the most advanced capitalist countries the trade unions are now stepping beyond the narrow field of wage claims and concerning themselves not only with working conditions but with social policy as a whole, the problems originally subsumed under the label 'incomes policy' are becoming broader and much more complicated. These problems can be tackled adequately only by systematic consultation between government and the unions in the context of what is usually called planning policy. Nor should these consultations cover merely wages and prices policy, or indeed stop at general economic policy; they should extend to social policy, or what in Italy is called reform policy. In Italy, indeed, the tendency of trade unions to assert their bargaining power in social policy is more pronounced than in other capitalist countries, and the antagonism between the old and the new, in the economy and in the entire social fabric, is very bitter. The signs are plain for all to see: unless the government manages to put through some essential reforms, there is a danger of mounting social conflict. There may be some relaxation, to be sure, at times of slackening economic growth, when rising unemployment and underemployment weakens the unions' bargaining power. But this is a high price to pay: if growth falters, the workers are not the only ones to be hurt, but the whole nation suffers in one way or another.

Whatever happens, whether the pace of economic growth keeps up its momentum or whether it slackens, some inflationary pressure is unavoidable. It is a built-in feature of the modern industrial society, whose structure is the result of the concentration of firms, which in turn has technological roots, and of the related growing strength of the trade unions. In the last analysis, inflationary pressure today derives from the large firms' power to set prices via the control of production, and from the big unions' power to influence wages. These two structural features are in some countries, including Italy, flanked by two others, which probably cannot rightly be described as structural; they are the relatively low and only slowly increasing efficiency of retail trade, and the inability of legislation and public intervention to restrain the rise in the price of building land as well as to add as quickly to the stock of low-cost housing as the pace of urbanisation requires.

The two structural features are common to all capitalist industrial countries; so are the two others, but in greatly varying measure. It follows that the problem of inflation is not a domestic one for each individual country. Both price rises and wage rises are in some way a response to international pressures.

If structural inflation, as evident in the cost of living, is to be kept down to 2 to 2·5 per cent, this can be done (and even then only by great exertions) only provided world prices for finished products and raw materials keep reasonably stable. If they are on a rising trend, the target has to be formulated in other terms. Domestic prices would then have to be prevented from rising faster than international wholesale prices, especially those of manufactures (lest international competitiveness be eroded), and a 2−2·5 per cent limit would have to be imposed on the divergence between the rates of increase in the cost of living and in wholesale prices, although in periods of rapid inflation wholesale prices may rise faster than the cost of living.

It is hard to tell what the future holds. All things considered, it seems unlikely that international wholesale prices will remain tendentially stable in the years to come. Nearly all industrial countries are in a situation of more or less full employment, so that an upward pressure on prices deriving from wages outpacing productivity is likely to occur more often than in the past.

7 Raw material prices and decreasing returns

Looking further ahead, there seems even more reason for concern about international prices. We had all got used to discard as mistaken Ricardo's views about the strength of the tendency towards decreasing returns in respect of technical progress. The algebraic sum which Ricardo took to be negative, has instead turned out to be decidedly positive, in the sense that technical progress has proved capable of offsetting the decreasing returns and still leaving a positive margin, so that in effect the returns from land and mines were increasing rather than decreasing. But now it looks as though it was not Ricardo who was wrong, but we, and that we would do well to revise our views and return to his. There are some resources for which demand has begun to rise faster than supply, over more than short periods. In 1973, with a general boom in the capitalist countries, the supply of many raw materials fell short of demand and all their prices exploded simultaneously at unprecedented rates; and there are signs that the developing countries which produce these raw materials are beginning to organise themselves with a view to reaping more than ephemeral advantages from this propitious situation. Very probably it will not last. Once the boom is over, raw material prices can be expected to fall back to their previous levels. Nevertheless, we must envisage the possibility that the circumstances we are now witnessing are but the forerunners of a much more lasting, or indeed chronic, situation which might well come about in the not too distant future. The spread and speed of development processes have raised demand for raw materials to such an extent that we must expect a growing shortage of some of the principal ones. The self-same technical progress which for so long more than offset nature's decreasing returns by its effect on supply, may now, through its effect on demand, cause them to reappear. And if the Rome Club's gloomy prognosis regarding the progressive exhaustion of many natural resources should prove to be right, then, clearly, the world's advanced countries must expect obstacles to expansion which are bound to generate inflationary pressures of mounting gravity. If raw material prices rise faster than the prices of finished products, one can foresee a fall in profits to the detriment of the process of accumulation, just as Ricardo said. If such events came to pass, one result among many might well be that developing countries would find their bargaining power steadily increasing, and this would herald profound change in the underlying trends governing the economy of the world's different countries.

Notes

[1] More precisely, in England during the first half of the nineteenth century, money wages oscillated around an almost stationary level, and real wages rose very slowly as a result of the long-run price fall. Both in England and in the United States, during the second half of the century real wages rose as a result partly of the rising trend of money wages, and partly of a fall in prices, especially food prices.

[2] In industry prices fell relatively little, but in agriculture (which by then accounted for a relatively small proportion of total income) there was a sharp price fall, accompanied by virtually stationary production and

rising employment, due to a return flow of manpower to the land.

[3] See *Relazione della Banca d'Italia per il 1964*, p.64. According to Thirlwall and Barton ('Inflation and growth: the international evidence' *Banca nazionale del lavoro Quarterly Review*, September 1971) inflation stimulates expansion provided it keeps within certain limits (8—10 per cent).

[4] For the period 1953—61, in Italy, the rank correlation coefficient for productivity increases and the degree of concentration in industry (13 sectors) was about +0·8.

[5] By 'industry' is meant a group of products interrelated either by the characteristics of demand or by technology, in which latter case the linkage may be vertical, as between different stages of the production process, or horizontal, as between joint or related products.

Appendix Table 3.1
Prices, wages and productivity in Italy.
Annual average rates of change, per cent[a]

		1952–1961	1961–1970	1970–1971
1.	*Wholesale prices*			
	(i) Domestic	− 0·2	+ 2·6	+ 4·2
	agricultural	+ 1·0	+ 3·5	+ 4·9
	industrial	− 0·7	+ 2·7	+ 4·0
	(ii) International			
	agricultural	− 1·9	+ 2·1	+ 3·3
	industrial	+ 0·6	+ 1·9	+ 3·8
	raw materials	− 0·1	+ 1·6	+ 3·0
2.	*Cost of living*	+ 2·7	+ 4·2	+ 5·3
	consumer prices	+ 2·8[b]	+ 4·2	+ 5·3
	goods	+ 1·3[b]	+ 3·3	+ 5·3
	services	+ 4·8[b]	+ 5·5	+ 5·3
	dwellings[c]	+ 16·6	+ 7·6	+ 3·9
3.	*Money wages*[d]			
	agriculture	+ 3·9	+ 11·9	+ 15·9
	industry	+ 4·1	+ 10·0	+ 10·6
	trade	+ 4·2	+ 7·9	+ 12·5
4.	*Real wages in industry*	+ 1·4	+ 5·9	+ 5·0
5.	*Salaries of public employees*[e]			
	in money terms	+ 3·4	+ 7·8	+ 5·8
	in real terms	+ 0·7	+ 3·6	+ 0·4
6.	*Private salaries*			
	in money terms	+ 4·4	+ 8·9	+ 9·4
	in real terms	+ 1·7	+ 4·7	+ 3·9
7.	*Productivity of labour*			
	agriculture	+ 5·5	+ 6·9	+ 4·2
	industry	+ 6·6	+ 6·5	+ 2·1
	trade[f]	+ 2·4	+ 3·1	+ 4·0

Sources: For all figures except those under 1 (ii), agricultural and industrial,
the Yearbook and Bulletin of the Italian Central Institute of Statistics, the
Ministry of Labour's Labour Statistics, and the annual General Report on
the Economic Situation of the Country prepared by the Ministry of the Budget. For the international prices of agricultural and industrial products,
United Nations, *Statistical Yearbook* and *Monthly Statistical Bulletin*.

Notes to Table 3.1

a My thanks are due to Dr Carlo Del Monte, who compiled the data, made the calculations and gave me the benefit of his valuable advice.

b Period 1953–1961.

c For the period 1952–1961: increases used in the old cost-of-living index (1938 = 100), which is similar to that relevant for the escalator clause. This latter index takes account only of dwellings subject to rent control, but the rents of which were gradually decontrolled during the period – which explains the high rate of increase. Actually, free rents rose as well, but not so fast; it may be assumed that their rate of increase was just a little lower than that shown for the years 1961–1970. For the latter period, the figures are based on the new cost-of-living indices, whose composition was changed three times: in 1961, 1966 and again in 1970. For rents, the new indices are based on a weighted average of controlled and free rents. The rate of increase appears much slower in this second period than in the preceding one, partly for purely statistical reasons, as indicated, and partly because the real effect of the relaxation of rent control was much weaker.

d Minimum contractual wages excluding family allowances. When considering periods covering several years, as is done here, the rates of change (not the levels) of minimum contractual wages are very close to the rates of change in actual earnings, which include all social charges, bonuses and other extras. (For example, the annual average rates of increase in hourly earnings in industry, during the periods 1952–1961 and 1961–1970 respectively, were 4·7 and 9·6 per cent, compared with 4·1 and 10 per cent rises in minimum contractual wages). However, it must be remembered that while these rates of change are fairly significant with reference to modern firms, they are not significant with reference to very small firms such as abound in building, the clothing industry and engineering workshops. Yet small firms employ a very considerable proportion of the labour force (some 40 per cent of all workers in industry are employed by firms with total personnel of less than ten). Sometimes, especially in Southern Italy, these small firms do not even pay contractual wage rates, and to this end resort to expedients which may be formally legal (e.g. employment of apprentices and home workers) or, for that matter, illegal (employment of minors). In these small firms wage rises are lagged and in any case much smaller than required by the contract.

e Until 1968, the salaries of public employees, category B; from 1969, average salaries in public administration. In both cases, minimum contractual pay excluding family allowances.

f While in productive sectors productivity is understood as the ratio of the volume of output to number of persons employed, in trade it is expressed by the ratio of the quantity of goods sold to consumers ('private consumption') to the number of persons employed in trade.

Table 3.2

The share of profits in the gross product of
manufacturing industry in Italy, 1951 to 1972[a]

1951	113·3	1962	100·3
1952	104·8	1963	96·2
1953	100·0	1964	91·1
1954	105·1	1965	92·0
1955	109·8	1966	97·3
1956	109·3	1967	91·4
1957	109·6	1968	93·8
1958	105·5	1969	91·3
1959	113·9	1970	88·9
1960	114·3	1971	77·6
1961	110·6	1972	83·1

Sources: Istituto nazionale per lo studio della congiuntura (ISCO), National accounts for the period 1951 to 1971; Ministry of the Budget, Report on the Economic Situation of the Country, 1972.

Note: [a] Indices calculated by the formula $\dfrac{VA - W}{VA}$, where VA is value added and W is wages and salaries.

4 Investment, Productivity and Financial Policy in Italy during the Sixties

I Investment and productivity

1 *The economic effects of investment*

Investment has three kinds of effects: it increases demand, productive capacity, and productivity (output per man or, in industry, per man-hour). The first effect, which is the one Keynes was most interested in, occurs during the same period as the investment itself; the other two come later.

Given the propensity to consume, the increase in demand depends on the *volume* of investment; the increase in productive capacity and in productivity, on the other hand, depends both on the volume and *type* of investment, as well as on the organisational pattern of the production process regarding such matters as working schedules, the distribution of jobs and the number of extra shifts worked. Changes in employment, therefore, depend jointly on changes in aggregate demand, on the type of investment and on changes in the organisation of production. Keynes and his followers focused the limelight on the investment–demand–employment relationship and paid little attention to the effects of the type of investment and the organisation of production. In speaking of different types of investment I have in mind not merely the fact that a road or a dam is nothing like, say, the installation of a new machine in a factory; rather, I am concerned with the effects of new machines themselves on the technical coefficients of production function. Some machines which replace or are added to existing ones do little or nothing to alter the coefficients, others alter them very considerably. Changes in technical coefficients, it will be recalled, do not enter at all into Keynesian theory in its original form. As regards changes in the way work is organised, which usually, though not necessarily, follow new investment, this is a matter to which no economists, Keynesians or non-Keynesians, have paid much attention, with the sole exception of Marxists. Even they, however, never went beyond the most general observations.

123

2 Industrial investment in Italy during the last twenty years

Let us examine what happened in Italy during the last twenty years and what relationships can be detected between investment, productivity and employment, with special reference to industry.

During the fifties industrial investment, at constant prices, grew at an annual average rate of no less than 7·3 per cent. In the sixties, the picture was very different. A two-year spurt in 1962 and 1963 was followed by six years, 1964 to 1969, during which industrial investment as a whole did not expand. In sharp contrast, hourly productivity increased at an almost unchanged rate right through these three periods; capital per worker employed increased at virtually identical rates during the first and the third period (interrupted by a big spurt during the 1961–63 boom); and output expanded at closely similar rates during the first and the second period, but more slowly since then. The relevant annual average rates of change are tabulated below.[1]

	1951–61	1962–63	1964–69
Investment	+ 7·3	+ 12·0	0
Hourly productivity	+ 6·4	+ 6·7	+ 6·4
Capital per worker	+ 4·1	+ 8·2	+ 4·2
Output	+ 8·2	+ 8·6	+ 6·9

Industrial investment plunged by 37 per cent in the two-year period 1964 to 1965 and then rose so slowly that it took until 1969 to get back to the 1963 level.

What was the reason for this drastic fall in industrial investment after 1963? And why was it that, nevertheless, industrial output and productivity continued to rise at much the same, or only a moderately slower, rate than before?

The two questions are interrelated, and so, therefore, are the answers. But it will be well to discuss them separately, for the sake of clarity and also in an attempt at identifying the various forces at work.

3 Investment-depressing factors

Three kinds of factors are usually held responsible for the poor investment performance after 1963. They are political factors; wage rises ahead of productivity, which squeezed profit margins, one of the determinants of investment; and the effects of financial and credit policy. All three sets of factors were relevant, but, as I shall try to show, the intensity of their effects on investment varied in different years.

The influences hardest to pinpoint are, of course, those of political factors.

No process of social transformation and no shift in the political balance ever happens without a price having to be paid for it. There can be no doubt that the formation of the centre-left government at first gave rise to strong misgivings among industrialists, especially after the nationalisation of electricity, which deprived the private sector of one of its financial strongholds.[2] In point of fact, the nationalised electricity companies were given generous, indeed overgenerous compensation; but when the instalments were paid out, the loan issues which financed them swamped the bond market,[3] and the money was only in small part used for productive investment, while the bulk of it went into speculative investment in real estate and distribution (see Postcript to this chapter).

These are only some of the political factors which depressed investment. There is reason to believe that the effect of political factors was strong during the first two years of the centre-left government, in 1963 and 1964, much weaker during the following three years, and strong once more in 1969 and 1970, this time because of the instability and precarious nature of successive governments. This influence is still at work. However, good or bad, the influence of political factors defies measurement and hence rigorous analysis. The other two kinds of factors do lend themselves to more precise logical and chronological analysis based on quantitative observation. Let us look, therefore, at industrial investment with reference to these two factors.

4   *The investment slump of 1964*

The steep fall of investment in 1964 is not difficult to explain. In line with the propositions developed in Chapter 1 (Section 7), I assume three determinants of industrial investment: the share of gross profits in the total of value added in industry, total liquidity (as an index of the supply of finance funds external to the firm), and the degree of unused capacity.

The profit share started to decline as of 1961, and this must presumably have played a part in slowing down the rate of investment growth, even though the absolute level of industrial investment did not actually fall until 1964 (and again in 1965). However, while declining profits depressed investment during the years 1961 to 1963, an opposite, upward influence came from expanding consumption demand, via a decreasing degree of unused capacity. The net effect of these two opposite influences was still positive so far as the absolute volume of investment is concerned, but negative with respect to its rate of increase. In 1962 and 1963 the fall in the profit share became much steeper, because wage rises far outpaced productivity gains and prices absorbed only part of the additional labour cost. At this stage the fall in profits definitely held back investment growth. But the *coup de grâce* came from the credit restrictions introduced by the Bank of Italy during the last quarter of 1963, chiefly with a view to stopping, and indeed reversing, the mounting deficit in external payments. This purpose was achieved in the second half of 1964; a sharp contraction of demand for home-produced and foreign capital goods led, via a multiplier mechanism, to a slow-down of the increase in demand for home-produced and foreign consumer goods as well. But the cost, in terms of economic growth, was high. Industrial investment dropped by more than 20 per cent in 1964. Granted that the chief error of monetary policy was committed earlier − in 1962 and the first half of 1963, when the foot was pressed down on the accelerator too hard − there is no gainsaying that now the brake was applied too sharply.

What happened after 1964 is much more difficult to interpret. Why was it that industrial investment picked up so slowly that it took five years, until 1969, to regain its 1963 level?

5 Investment after 1964

In 1965, industrial investment still had not shaken off the effects of the severe credit squeeze introduced late in 1963. Moreover profits, which had shrunk for some years, and most of all in 1964, hardly picked up at all.

The profit share reached a peak in 1960−61 and then touched bottom in 1964. Thereafter it rose slowly and by no means continuously and it seems that no significant recovery took place before 1966 (see Table 4.2 below). Almost immediately there followed another decline in 1967, this time because of the discontinuation of the system by which part of the employers' social charges were paid by the state.

Throughout almost the whole of the period under consideration, therefore, profits certainly must be counted as an investment-depressing factor. Since firms earned little, they could step up investment only by drawing more heavily on outside funds, that is, bank credit and the issue of bonds and shares. Share issues could not be expected to contribute much, because the stock market was in the dumps, not only for reasons of taxation but precisely because profit margins were so slim.[4] This left more to be taken care of by bank credits and bond issues, two sources of funds which are not entirely substitutable, since bank credits are used for working capital and for prefinancing medium- and long-term investment subsequently to be paid for out of the proceeds of bond issues. In any event, only fairly large companies can raise money on bonds; small firms, when they need outside funds beyond trade credits from suppliers, have access only to bank credit and subsidised credit. State-controlled enterprises got conspicuous sums in some years by additional appropriations to their endowment fund.

In all, credit assumed growing importance in the course of the years under consideration. It remains to be seen whether there was enough of it to meet all requirements. As regards incentives to invest, there was little encouragement from the side of profit, and there was a case, therefore, for strengthening those on the side of demand. Government can influence demand via public finance policy, and it can also directly influence the total volume of industrial investment through the investment policy of public enterprises, which, during the period concerned, accounted for 30 to 50 per cent of total investment in industry. Let us look at this aspect first, before going on to examine public finance policy as such, as well as monetary and credit policy.

Table 4.1

Industrial investment at constant prices, 1964 to 1969
(rates of change, per cent)

| Year | Public enterprises | | Private enterprises | Total |
	State-controlled	Total		
1964	− 7·9	− 3·9	− 28·8	− 20·1
1965	− 24·5	− 14·7	− 25·1	− 20·7
1966	− 21·0	− 11·6	+ 28·6	+ 10·4
1967	+ 0·8	+ 7·1	+ 16·3	+ 13·1
1968	+ 14·2	+ 11·1	+ 10·4	+ 10·7
1969	+ 24·9	+ 16·8	+ 5·0	+ 11·0

Source: Annual Report of the Bank of Italy, and General Report on the Economic Situation of the Country, successive years.

Counting as public enterprises state-controlled companies, municipal undertakings and the National Electricity Board, the dismaying fact is that their total investment expenditure declined just when for reasons of countercyclical policy it should have gone up. The figures of Table 4.1 (which exclude residential building), are eloquent. It remains to discover just why public-enterprise investment contracted in the years 1964 to 1967.

A number of explanations have been put forward: (1) several big investment projects, especially in steel (the Taranto works) and in cement had just reached completion; (2) some investment projects initiated when demand was growing rapidly, were scaled down in the face of slower or nil growth of demand for many industrial products; (3) the propensity to invest declined because of the shrinking supply both of self-financing and outside funds. With regard to self-financing capacity, it has been argued that in public enterprises, which cannot so readily pass cost increases on to prices, the decline of profits was heavier than in private ones. And as for borrowing, one could often hear the strange argument in those years that public enterprises must not raise funds to the detriment of private ones,[5] or in other words that the requirements of private firms should have prior claims on such funds as the capital market was able to supply. Nobody knows to what extent this odd principle was actually put into practice, but all in all public enterprises certainly got little new money from 1965 to 1967, apart from a number of increases in their endowment funds; even these sometimes brought in no hard cash for quite a while, inasmuch as they were appropriated but not paid out. The truth is that, while in 1964 and some part of 1965 it was up to a point reasonable enough to explain the sluggish investment of public enterprises in terms of the completion of some big projects and the downward revision of others planned during the boom, this certainly does not apply to the subsequent years. At that time there really seems to be no other explanation than that the government was deliberately keeping down industrial investment by public enterprises so as to prevent them from competing for funds on the capital market with private firms. It seems reasonable to suppose that this policy was designed to reassure the latter after the trauma of the nationalisation of the electricity industry and, more generally, to demonstrate the friendly intentions of the centre-left government towards private enterprise. In any event, there is little doubt that in those years public-enterprise investment not only failed to counteract the recession but actually did much to prolong it and to retard recovery. From 1968 on, however, the picture changed radically (see Table 4.1, and also the Postscript to this chapter).

II   Financial policy, employment and inflation

6   *The public-sector deficit*

Italy's public finances during the years 1965 to 1969 were dominated by the conspicuous and growing deficit of the public sector. Generally speaking, such a deficit can be financed either by the creation of money or by security issues, or, most often and certainly during the period under consideration, in both ways (see Table 4.2 below). What was the effect of this deficit on economic growth? Did it act as a stimulus or as a brake?

By and large, the public deficit had the effect of holding back growth. Let us see why.

A public deficit can be financed without any detriment at all to the coverage of the private sector's financial requirements so long as any money created and any securities issued for the purpose are additional to the money that would have been created, and the securities that would have been issued, in the absence of the public deficit. But if the new money or the new securities, or both, are not entirely additional, then the coverage of the public deficit makes, to that extent, inroads into the finance funds available for the private sector.

Since 1965, when the public sector's deficit assumed really large proportions, we had in Italy a sort of planning of monetary flows, in which the public-sector deficit appears as the primary constraint. Every year, the monetary authorities fix in advance two upper limits: an upper limit to monetary base creation, beyond which there would be a serious risk of inflation (or of speeding up the pace of existing inflation), and an upper limit to security issues (for the sake of simplicity, I refer only to fixed-interest securities), beyond which there would be a serious risk of a collapse of bond prices.

If, in such conditions, the public deficit and the presumed requirements of the private sector add up to more than the sum of the pyramid of bank credit that can be built up over the maximum allowable monetary base plus maximum allowable security issues, then indeed the public deficit can be covered only by leaving part of the private sector's requirements unsatisfied. The higher the public deficit and the more cautious the determination of the two maximum limits, the greater, of course, is the likelihood of conflict in the coverage of public and private requirements. And it is easier to err in setting the limit to additional monetary base creation, because in the case of securities there are fairly accurate objective indications regarding the absorptive capacity of the capital market. In setting a limit to money creation, the only yardstick is the total volume of disposable productive resources; from this one can estimate how much scope there is for expanding output and monetary assets without detriment to (relative) price stability and (relative) equilibrium in external payments. But, as we shall see presently, such estimates are unusually hazardous, especially *ex ante*; with the benefit of hindsight one can speak with rather more assurance. Today, with the information now at hand, we can say that in several of the years under consideration the monetary authorities probably fixed too low a ceiling for additional money creation, or, what comes to the same thing, that they considerably underestimated the scope for expansion subject to the constraints of price stability and external balance. The result was an unnecessary aggravation of the conflict between the rival claims for coverage of the public deficit and the private sector's financial requirements. In the end effect, therefore, the monetary authorities in those years exercised a no doubt unintended restrictive influence on investment in the private sector and more especially, from 1965 to 1967, on investment by state-controlled enterprises.[6] In any event, the likelihood of conflict in the coverage of public and private requirements is heightened by the manner of application of the constitutional principle that funds must actually be at hand before they may be spent. In practice there is usually some delay between the public sector's fund-raising and its expenditure, so that public bond issues have a deflationary effect during the interval in which they withdraw purchasing power from circulation, and certainly reduce the potential funds available for the medium- and long-term financing of the private sector.

Without taking the analysis any further, I do wish to draw attention to some indications which suggest that the problem of conflict in the coverage of the public and the private sector's requirements ought to be taken very seriously indeed.

In updating to 1968 the equation for unused capacity in the econometric model of the Italian economy presented in Chapter 1, I found that one of the coefficients of correlation, as well as other characteristics, were rather unsatisfactory — certainly less satisfactory than in the original estimate for the period 1951–1965. In the original equation, the degree of unused capacity depended on the principal components of total demand for industrial products — that is, private consumption, investment and industrial exports; the explanatory variables were expressed in terms of rates of change. In updating the equation I made several tests; among others, I included the public borrowing requirement (which became very large after 1965) on the Keynesian assumption that an increase in the budget deficit helps to reduce the degree of unused capacity. To my surprise I found that the public-debt coefficient was not negative, but positive, which suggests that, other things being equal, an increase in the public debt should raise rather than reduce the degree of unused capacity. This was altogether against expectations. Assuming that the relation is genuine and not merely incidental, the explanation probably lies in that very conflict that can arise in the coverage of the public deficit and the private sector's financial requirements — a conflict which may perhaps in part be attributed to the general principles governing control of finance flows. The Keynesian hypothesis certainly holds good when deficit spending is wholly, or predominantly, financed by additional money and securities; otherwise, the effect of deficit spending on income and on the degree of capacity utilisation may be negative.[7]

Here, then, we have a first indication. Another can be found in the figures for monetary base creation and money supply, which, for the years 1964—1967, give evidence of a manifestly restrictive policy (Table 4.2).

Looking at the figures for 1964 and 1965, we find monetary base creation stepped up from 952 to 1,339 billion lire, and the money supply growing even more, from 2,016 to 3,876 billion. But it must be remembered that this followed two years of severe restriction, so that the 1965 increases only just brought the two series back to the trend (in 1962 monetary base creation was 1,242 and the increase money supply 2,930 billion lire). In 1965 and in 1969 a very modest increase in the monetary base was associated with a fairly conspicuous expansion of the money supply, presumably because in these two years the new rules regarding securities admissible as reserve assets made their effect. However, in 1969 the increases all occurred in the first half of the year; during the third and fourth quarter policy again switched very decidedly to credit restrictions, for reasons having to do not only with the budget deficit, but also with mounting capital exports, in turn due, among other things, to the increasing differential between interest rates at home and abroad.[8] That leaves only one year, 1968, of decidedly expansionary monetary and credit policy. I would argue that throughout the sixties, and especially from 1964 to 1967, the total volume of short-term credit at most times expanded slowly because of the relatively slow increase in medium- and long-term credits, and that this relative slowness was due mainly to financial policy.

The bank of Italy officially supported bond prices from 1966 to 1969 (and in fact had started doing so already in 1965). The main purpose was to make it easier to place bond issues with the public. Since the Bank stood ready to buy any amount of bonds at the day's price, this might have caused the monetary base to expand without foreseeable limits, a potentially highly inflationary process. During the period under consider-

Table 4.2

Profits, money creation and net bond issues in Italy, 1954 to 1969
(billion lire, except col. 1)

Years	Index of profit share in manu- facturing industry	Monetary base creation	Increase in money supply	Treasury cash deficit	Net issues of bonds†			Shares
					state†	private sector	total	
1954–57*	108·5	368	800	432	211	194	405	159
1958–59*	109·6	933	1500	502	180	406	586	224
1960–63*	105·4	765	2500	519	87	926	1013	531
1964–69*	92·8	1191	4500	1521	1057	1470	2527	501
1964	91·1	952	2016	817	228	1234	1462	581
1965	92·0	1339	3876	1545	679	1306	1985	406
1966	97·3	1239	4012	1823	1568	1279	2847	470
1967	91·4	1154	4108	1226	1012	1419	2431	396
1968	93·8	1221	5183	2022	1297	1795	3092	473
1969	91·3	1245	4827	1692	1550	1790	3350	681

* Annual averages.
† Excluding Treasury Bills.

132

ation, this risk was avoided precisely by the advance rationing of new issues and, more generally, by planning of financial flows. Actually, if I am right in thinking that this planning was too strict, the effect was not only to eliminate inflationary risks, but, so far as investment is concerned, to exercise a restrictive or, at the very least, not sufficiently stimulating influence.

In reviewing the Bank's price stabilisation policy, the Annual Report for 1969 admits, with praiseworthy frankness, that monetary policy might have been 'more aggressive' (Abridged English Version, p. 190):

> Of the two purposes of the stabilisation policy, one, the creation of a broader market for bonds, was by and large achieved. ... The aim of stimulating investment was achieved only in part; a more aggressive policy might have been desirable, but it would have been imprudent to implement it by lowering the level of interest rates even further.

Now, it must be pointed out that that policy could have been made more aggressive without depressing the level of interest rates; at least in some years, it would have been perfectly possible both to create more money (for financing the public deficit) and to allow more bond issues (for financing productive investment, especially by public enterprises). Even granted the case for stable bond prices, what could and should have been done is to balance the two increases in the right proportions – the increase, that is, in the quantity of money, which has a bearing on the demand for securities, and the increase in the volume of new issues, keeping in mind that an increase in the quantity of money tends to depress yields, while an increase in the supply of securities tends to raise them.[9]

But not only monetary and credit policy was, at least until 1967, dominated by an excessive fear of inflation; the same is true of the whole of financial policy. At first sight this statement seems to be contradicted by the rapidly mounting public deficit after 1964, which suggests that the public administration had too high a propensity to spend.

But the contradiction is apparent only, for several reasons.

Table 4.2

Sources: For the profit share see Table 3.2. The other figures are taken from the Bank of Italy's Annual Reports. Those for the money supply are the sum of primary and secondary liquidities, that is: notes and coin, current bank accounts and current Post Office accounts, plus savings and other deposits at banks, Post Office savings books and certificates, Treasury Bills and deposits with the Treasury. The monetary base comprises all the legal tender plus the monetary authorities' short-term liabilities which the banks can use as obligatory reserves; it also includes those short-term assets which, although they cannot be used as reserves, can at the holders' request directly and rapidly give rise to the creation of fresh legal tender money. (Banca d'Italia, *Abridged Version of the Report for the Year 1967*, Rome 1968, p. 91).

First of all, the government's financial policy has to do not only with revenue and expenditure, but with other important matters, including the investment projects of public enterprises — and these projects, as we have seen, got into financial difficulties at least in the years 1965, 1966 and 1967, precisely because of the government's policy. Secondly, if there is justification for criticising the strict manner in which the deficit was financed, it is reasonable to suppose that more liberal financing methods would have led to a more rapid expansion of investment, income and ultimately public revenue, so that, at equal expenditure growth, the deficit would have been smaller. Finally, the deficit cannot be treated in isolation, but must be seen in relation to the degree of resource utilisation and to the balance of payments. One cannot but subscribe to what the Governor of the Bank of Italy himself said in the Annual Report for 1967 (p. 361 of the Italian version — cf., for the context, p. 162 of the Abridged English Version):

> The economic system could have stood more public expenditure, or, with less taxation, could have generated proportionately more private expenditure, without the appearance of any harmful strains. On the side of real resources, increased demand could have been met by the fuller use of existing production capacity and by a reduction in the balance-of-payments surplus on current account; and from the monetary point of view, the creation of additional liquidity for financing a higher budget deficit would, at least in part, have been offset by less liquidity creation originating in the foreign sector. [10]

It is my considered opinion that Italy's economic policy makers underestimated the scope for growth subject to the constraints of price stability and of external balance, and that they did so not only in 1967 but also in other years during the period under consideration. And because of this underestimation, the public deficit was financed in such a way as to curtail the expansion of finance funds for the private sector more than was necessary, and financial policy as a whole failed to give enough stimulus to growth or was downright restrictive.

The very composition of the deficit is open to criticism, in that the deficit was due largely to current expenditure rising faster than current revenue, while investment spending marked time and, in three of the six years under discussion, actually contracted (see Table 4.3).

One can hear it said that public investment expenditure grows slowly because of the public administration's notorious inefficiency. This is true enough, but it does not tell the whole story. This inefficiency is a constant, and a constant cannot explain the remarkable differences in the

Table 4.3

Public sector: revenue and expenditure, 1954 to 1969
(rates of change, per cent)

Years	Current revenue	Current expenditure	Capital expenditure		
			Investment	Transfers	Total
1954–57*	12·1	10·7	8·0	11·3	6·5
1958–59*	8·4	10·3	5·9	−12·2	−0·5
1960–63*	13·6	13·0	8·5	6·2	10·1
1964–69*	10·2	11·9	−5·4	21·4	9·6
1964	12·5	11·3	16·8	6·0	13·8
1965	7·2	17·8	−4·1	75·5	16·2
1966	7·7	9·0	8·0	− 6·8	2·3
1967	14·9	8·9	−2·6	39·5	12·2
1968	9·8	12·3	22·3	− 1·3	12·0
1969	9·4	12·3	−7·3	15·3	1·4

* Annual averages.

Sources: National Institute for Business Cycle Research (ISCO), National Accounts 1951–1968, Rome 1970; General Report on the Economic Situation of the Country, 1970.

rates of change. This explanation, for instance, throws no light at all on the spurts in 1964 and 1968; these were due to political decisions, which obviously were not frustrated by the public administration's inefficiency. It is true that when public investment spending declined, capital transfers (loans and subsidies, including increases in the endowment funds of public enterprises) rose, so that total capital expenditure changed only within narrow limits, and always upward. But this only confirms, from another angle, that public investment expenditure is always flexible in the sense that it can not merely be reduced, but increased as well, at least with reference to a one-year period. Admittedly, it needs several months to step up investment expenditure in any appreciable measure, and even then only on condition that investment projects are ready or almost ready; otherwise the interval between a spending decision and actual disbursement of money is bound to be very much longer. (To this extent it may be justified to speak of slowness and inefficiency in connection with investment expenditure, but one should take care not to impute to this also the consequences of deliberate political choices). By contrast, this interval can be quite short in the case of current expenditure and capital transfers; if Parliament appropriates a sum for the increase in a government-controlled company's endowment fund, this can be paid out quite quickly, and of course current expenditure too can be adjusted without losing much time.

The conspicuous ups and downs in the rate of change of public investment expenditure during the period considered prove one thing beyond doubt, and this is that the government's investment policy was haphazard and contradictory. It cannot even be argued that investment spending was in some years reduced *because* of current expenditure running away as a result of decisions taken under political pressure which the government was too weak to resist. This is simply not true, or at least not in all the years under consideration. The very opposite happened in some years, when the government seems to have overreacted to inflation fears and tried to contain the growth of both current and capital spending, only to find later that it was possible and indeed expedient to spend more; but since investment expenditure could not be stepped up quickly within just a few months, certain current expenditures were speeded up instead. In these cases higher current spending was an effect rather than a cause of low investment. For instance, in 1966, 1967 and 1968 Italy's foreign exchange reserves grew to such an extent that some countries abroad began to press for a revaluation of the lira. The government swiftly responded with a very considerable increase in current expenditure, mainly via an immediately effective conspicuous rise in pensions; and this was done precisely because no quick reversal of investment policy was possible.

It would, then, have been perfectly possible for the deficit to grow less fast, or, if it grew at the same pace, to have had a different composition, allowing for less current and more investment expenditure. In that case the consequences, too, would have been very different, for two reasons. In the first place, public investment expenditure contributes, even if not immediately, to the growth of production capacity throughout the whole economy, and hence to the growth of income (and ultimately of tax revenue). Secondly, if the government had spent more on certain types of investment such as low-cost housing, schools, transport and hospitals, this would have taken some of the steam out of the social conflicts which followed and led to another, and stronger, wage explosion in 1969–1970.

It is no use crying over spilt milk, but at least we can try to learn from past errors and not to repeat the same or similar ones.

7 Money creation and the degree of resource utilisation

It has been suggested above that Italy's economic policy makers underestimated the scope for growth subject to the constraints of price stability and of external balance, and that because of this the public deficit was financed in such a way as to curtail the expansion of finance funds for the private sector more than was necessary. It remains to find out just how this unduly low estimate was arrived at.

According to Keynesian theory, deficit spending can and must be financed by additional monetary means when the country has unemployed productive resources — capacity and manpower. In the case of an open economy one must add the further condition of adequate currency reserves. Two of these three conditions certainly were met during the period under consideration; Italy had unused capacity and ample exchange reserves. Whether manpower resources really were underutilised is open to doubt.

Table 4.4

Degree of factor utilisation and exchange reserves in Italy, 1954 to 1969

Years	Degree of unused capacity in industry (per cent)	Non-agricultural unemployment (per cent)	End-year net total reserves (billion lire)
1964–57*	8·0	10·2	761
1958–59*	11·2	7·5	1687
1960–63*	5·0	4·0	1871
1964–69*	11·5	4·2	2900
1964	11·7	3·3	1838
1965	15·6	4·4	2743
1966	12·4	4·8	3067
1967	10·1	4·4	3294
1968	9·2	4·2	3500
1969	10·0	3·9	2958

* Annual averages.

Sources: For the first two columns, see the Appendix to Chapter 1; figures in the third column are from successive issues of the Bank of Italy's Bulletin.

The figures of Table 4.4 allow the conclusion that reserves were 'adequate', in terms both of import coverage and of steady growth up to 1969, when they fell as a result of mounting capital exports — but these need not be discussed in this context.

Estimates of the degree of unused capacity in industry are notoriously hazardous, but the jump from 5·0 per cent in 1960—1963 to 11·5 per cent for the period 1964—1969 here under consideration does at any rate show a sharply rising trend.

By contrast, the unemployment figures convey no clear message and are open to misinterpretation. At first sight the unemployment rate looks low during the period under consideration, due allowance made for Italian conditions. But the unemployment rate is an unreliable indicator of demand for labour. First of all there is, especially in Italy, little occupational and geographical mobility of labour, and secondly labour supply is not altogether independent of demand; when demand for labour rises, so does supply, and *vice versa*. Hence a policy of overall demand containment with a view to keeping down strains on the labour market and consequently also the pace of wage increases may well fail to achieve these very purposes, not to speak of its adverse effects on the growth of income and employment. It may happen that the level (or the rate of increase) of employment declines without any, or at least without a corresponding, diminution of recorded unemployment, for the members of the labour force with the highest demand elasticity (mostly women and very young men) simply withdraw from the market. Yet, in spite of weakness in the demand for labour and, to some extent, a decrease in labour supply, the trade unions may still press their wage claims, unless demand for labour not merely ceases to grow or goes into a gentle decline, but actually takes a plunge. But this can happen only in a prolonged depression.

8 *The decline of employment*

There has been much discussion and speculation recently on the reasons why total employment fell in Italy from 1961 on. There are 'optimists' who attribute the decline to physiological factors like young people staying longer at school, retirement at lower age, and withdrawal of women who can afford not to work. There is also a statistical reason, in that women who work on the land, though perhaps only seasonally, cease to be recorded as 'employed' when the family moves to a town. Then there are 'pessimists' who point out that employment fell both in the North and in the South, and in the same proportion — and nobody can pretend that living standards in the South are high. The employment rate in some southern areas was already very low by the standards of the more advanced regions; it had fallen from 35 per cent in 1961 to 33 per cent in 1969, and a further decrease must be regarded as a pathological symptom. Finally, the pessimists argue, the very fact that women, once off the land, disappear from the labour force also has its pathological aspect, in so far as it points to the rural women's low degree of education and scant skills.

Personally, I can see some truth in the optimists' arguments, but by and large feel that the pessimists are right. [11] Perhaps we can shed some light on the whole question by looking at the rates of change in employment in different sectors of the economy (Table 4.5).

Table 4.5

Average annual changes in employment by sectors, 1951 to 1969
(absolute figures, in thousands)

	1951−61	1962−63	1964−69
Agriculture	− 243	− 426	− 212
Industry	+ 184	+ 170	+ 10
Other activities	+ 134	+ 21	+ 77
Total	+ 75	− 235	− 125

Source: Central Statistical Institute, successive quarterly surveys of the labour force.

The years 1962 and 1963 are a special case; the figures for the flight from the land are so high, it seems, at least partly because of statistical adjustments following the 1961 census. But, comparing the eleven years 1951 to 1961 with the six years 1964 to 1969, it looks as though the fall in total employment is essentially attributable to industry's failure to absorb as many new workers as before. And this failure, in turn, would seem to be due jointly to the following two factors: (1) unsatisfactory investment in industry (an initial slump followed by very slow recovery), and (2) the delayed effect of the conspicuous wage increases of the years 1962, 1963 and 1964 on the demand for labour.

The first point is obvious enough, since the most sensitive part of demand for labour derives from demand for capital goods.

The second point requires more comment. It is reasonable to assume that when wages race ahead of productivity, firms will try to 'save' labour. Consequently, the composition of investment is bound to change; less money will be spent with a view to small and gradual changes in the coefficients of production, and more on automation and more generally labour-saving innovations in the production process.[12] Wage rises no doubt also speed up reorganisation of the production process; when they are very large, firms intensify working schedules, put on extra shifts and take other measures which put additional physical and nervous strain on the workers. [13] In other words, firms try to offset wage rises by productivity gains achieved thanks to changes in factory-floor organisation and in the composition — though not necessarily the volume — of investment. In any case, it may be difficult to step up the volume of investment if finance funds are in short supply, as indeed happened during the period under consideration.

The combined effect of wage rises and of the difficulties of raising outside funds led to reorganisation not only at the level of the firm, but at the level of whole branches of industry, which meant the disappearance of a good many of the smaller and least efficient firms, at least as independent units.

The interpretation briefly outlined above should help to explain the fall in industrial (and, as a result, total) employment in Italy during recent years. It also throws some light on another question which I raised earlier in this chapter (section 2), namely, why, in the years 1964 to 1969, hourly productivity in manufacturing industry continued to rise at much the same average rate and industrial output almost as much as before, while industrial investment came to a halt. Clearly, the expansion of output owed nearly everything to productivity gains, since employment remained all but stationary throughout the whole period; and there must have been a shift, in the composition of total investment, to labour-saving types.

My interpretation is compatible with two equations I recently put together; again I speak of compatibility rather than proof, because, quite apart from the reservations to which tests of this kind are always subject, I am bound to admit that my data, especially those relating to employment, are somewhat approximate and that I cannot be too sure about the economic significance of the results. We need more tests of the same kind in other countries, and only if they all tell more or less the same story shall we be able to trust them.

Anyway, here are the two equations. Both refer to the period 1951 to 1968; for the first of them, see also Chapter 2, section 18; for the second, see also Chapter 1, Postscript.

$$\dot{O}_i = 3{\cdot}052 + 0{\cdot}088\,\dot{I}_i - 0{\cdot}304\,\dot{W}_{i_{\tau-3}}$$
$$t = (4{\cdot}66) \quad (3{\cdot}68) \quad\ \ (4{\cdot}45) \tag{4.1}$$
$$R^2 = 0{\cdot}843 \qquad\qquad DW = 2{\cdot}375$$

$$\dot{I}_i = -71{\cdot}396 + 0{\cdot}751\,G - 2{\cdot}335\,UN + 1{\cdot}315\,\dot{L} + 1{\cdot}237\,\dot{W}_{i_{\tau-4}}$$
$$t = \quad (5{\cdot}00) \quad (6{\cdot}13) \qquad (8{\cdot}46) \qquad\ (4{\cdot}13) \qquad (7{\cdot}83) \tag{4.2}$$
$$R^2 = 0{\cdot}943 \qquad\quad DW = 2{\cdot}101$$

where $\dot{O}_i$ is the rate of change in industrial employment, $\dot{I}_i$ the rate of change in industrial investment, $\dot{W}_i$ the rate of change in industrial wages, G the share of gross profits in industry, UN the degree of unused capacity and $\dot{L}$ the rate of change in total liquidity. Note that in equation (4.1) (industrial employment) the rate of change in wages is lagged by three years and has a negative sign; in the second equation, it has a four-year lag and a positive sign. The first equation suggests that, other things being equal, a wage rise slows down employment growth. The second equation can be interpreted as follows: wages have a bearing not only on the composition of investment but, other things being equal, also on its volume — which means, *ceteris paribus*, a net positive effect of higher labour-saving investment on total investment. All this sounds plausible enough. But the time lags may seem a little odd; it seems that wage rises affect employment three years later, and industrial investment four years later (though in that case, too, a three-year lag is statistically significant). Perhaps this may seem more reasonable if we remember that the statistical data refer mainly to modern industry, where it certainly takes several years to give full effect to organisational changes and new investment.

9. Quantity theory and cost inflation

What has been said about employment, especially in industry, and about the degree of utilisation both of the labour force and plant, is directly relevant to the question as to whether it was right in Italy, in recent years, to pay so little heed to the Keynesian prescript about deficit spending — the prescript, that is, that the budget deficit ought to be financed by additional money and securities without any corresponding reduction in money creation and security issues for the private sector. In practice, it seems, this rule was largely disregarded in Italy. Instead, what happened was much more closely in line with the Friedman rule of money creation at a more or less constant rate, a rule infringed only to the extent of changes in the regulations specifying the securities admissible as reserve assets and other measures which, on the average, allowed secondary liquidities to expand more than primary ones.

These, at least, were the results, whatever the original intentions. There is something paradoxical about this line of conduct, inasmuch as the Bank of Italy had for some time past been a declared adherent of the theory of cost inflation. The puzzle is how this theory can be reconciled with the neo-quantitative approach.

On second thoughts, the paradox can perhaps be cleared up, at least in part, in the light of the Phillips relation between the level of unemployment and the rate of increase in money wages.

More precisely, it can be argued that effective demand — which, in the view of the Chicago School, varies with the money supply according to a fairly stable ratio — affects prices not only directly but indirectly as well, and that the indirect effects take the form of cost inflation. In this view cost-push is always secondary to the primary demand-pull.

Let us look more closely at this argument. It has been said that in the short period demand directly affects the wholesale prices of agricultural products, because, apart from support policies, competition is the prevailing market form in agriculture. The short-run effects of demand on wholesale industrial prices are of two kinds, both indirect. The first works via the degree of unused capacity, which, when it diminishes under the pressure of demand, tends to drive prices up; and the second via wages, which, when they rise more than productivity, raise labour costs which in turn drive prices up. It would follow that the pressure of demand works directly in the labour market, and indirectly in the market for goods.

There is some truth in this reasoning, but there are also some untenable propositions.

It is correct to say that demand directly affects agricultural prices, but so, in the opposite direction, does disposable supply (output plus net imports minus additions to stocks).

It is likewise correct to say that demand may affect the wholesale prices of industrial products via the degree of unused capacity, but it is correct only at very high capacity utilisation. And this, at least with reference to industry as a whole, is not a normal but an exceptional situation, since for various reasons most firms, especially if they are large, nearly always keep in hand some margin of unused capacity precisely in order to be able to cope with any abnormal expansion of demand. Large firms furthermore plan their investment in the light of the expected long-run expansion of demand (and with a view to discouraging new firms from entering the market), and as and when their investment projects mature, capacity grows almost uninterruptedly. On the other hand small firms of the kind

142

characteristic of near-competitive markets normally produce as much as they can (subject to seasonal variations) and invest with reference to a much shorter time horizon. When demand grows, therefore, the small firms' unused capacity is taken up very quickly and prices soon start rising. (In practice, this is often the situation in the industries making building materials, and this helps to explain the relative, in addition to the absolute, increase in house prices.) Finally, if it is true that demand affects agricultural prices, the food industry, at one remove only, soon feels the effect of rising demand and, hence, rising agricultural prices, in the form of a cost-push.

It is altogether wrong, on the other hand, to treat demand for labour in the same way as demand for goods in the name of the Phillips relation. Quite apart from one of John Stuart Mill's famous propositions, this is wrong for three reasons. First, it is now proved beyond doubt that wages vary in response not only to the degree of unemployment but also to changes in the cost of living. And in its turn the cost of living depends not only on the wholesale prices of agricultural and industrial commodities, but also on retail trade margins, on rents, fares, public utility charges and on other prices under public control; in all these cases the influence of labour costs is weak and indirect, if not totally absent. Secondly, the rate of increase in wages depends also on trade union militancy, which can be measured by the number of working hours or days lost through strikes. [14] Finally, as was pointed out in the preceding section, the degree of unemployment is at best only a partial — and, over a period of several years, an altogether misleading — indicator of the pressure of demand in the labour market.

It follows that the neo-quantitative approach and the theory of cost inflation are not compatible, or at any rate compatible only within a small area. Outside that area we find cost and price changes explicable in terms of one theory but not of the other.

The Bank of Italy in its Annual Reports never explicitly acknowledged its adherence to the Phillips relation and the prescripts deriving therefrom. But we do repeatedly find the argument that wage rises can become effective only if and when the central bank is willing to provide firms with enough money to pay them.

This argument is not borne out by the facts. Above-normal wage rises took place not only when the central bank's policy was permissive (as it was explicitly acknowledged to be in 1962 and the first half of 1963), but also when the central bank 'refused' to finance wage rises to the required extent, as happened in 1964 and in 1969 and 1970. The only appreciable slow-down in the pace of wage increases occurred in 1965, the second year of a fairly severe depression which certainly would have been worse still without the steady expansion of world demand and hence of exports. It really does take a true slump, with large-scale unemployment, to slow down the pace of wage rises. Therefore, above-normal wage rises are prevented not so much by the central bank's refusal to finance them, as by a very considerable weakening of the trade unions' bargaining position. I deliberately use the words 'very considerable', because, as we have seen, the rate of increase in wages is governed not only by the degree of unemployment, but also by other factors, which may on occasion exert opposing influences.

The argument described in the end effect constitutes only an apparent departure from the Phillips thesis. It really is a variant of it, and as such open to much the same criticism.

10   Demand inflation

The thesis that wage increases can become effective only when firms are provided with the money to finance them, is a more refined variant of the older thesis which holds that an increase in the money supply alone is a necessary, though not a sufficient, condition of a rise in prices. Both the old thesis and its more refined and modern variant find their logical expression in the eclectic argument that the distinction between demand-pull and cost-push inflation is in the last analysis an abstract one, and that, to the extent that it is valid at all, it is valid only for analytical purposes. In practice, it is argued, the two processes are indistinguishable, because cost increases can be transferred onto prices only in the presence of demand expansion.

It is high time to expose the error of this view. Even if it seldom happens in practice, it is perfectly possible for both the money supply and effective demand to decline at a time of rising prices. Analytically, this proposition raises some complex questions, for two reasons. First of all, money supply and effective demand do not necessarily change in the same proportion, nor indeed necessarily in the same direction; what counts, of course, is effective demand. Secondly, it clearly is misleading to talk in terms of the *general* level of prices. A distinction must be made between different categories of prices, with particular reference to the influences affecting retail prices and the cost of living, and bearing in mind that the rationale which explains changes in the wholesale prices of agricultural commodities and raw materials is different from that which explains changes in industrial prices. Yet the majority of economists carry on as though there were only one explanation for both in the short run, to wit, supply and demand.

As we have seen, changes in demand for industrial products entail corresponding changes in supply at unchanged prices. If prices change, they do so in response to changes in cost, especially direct cost. This proposition ceases to hold in only two cases. The first case is demand expansion greatly in excess of what the system has adapted itself to and is regarded as normal by producers (but then the assumption of constant cost is unrealistic). The second case is a considerable contraction of demand, but then total average costs rise even at constant factor prices, because of an increase in fixed cost per unit of output, so that, instead of falling, prices may rise – as indeed has happened more than once.

Note that the above proposition links up with a similar Keynesian one, which, in modern conditions of industrial structure, is valid not only in periods of depression, as Keynes thought, but also in periods of expansion, so long as it proceeds at a 'normal' rate. The assumption that industrial (wholesale) prices are generally not affected by demand changes fits in with the following facts.

1   During the period 1952 to 1961 demand for industrial products in Italy rose rapidly, yet prices declined slightly (because costs declined, especially labour costs).

2   During the period from September–November 1963 to the first quarter of 1965 demand for many industrial products decreased, as shown by output figures; yet, because of a cost increase, wholesale prices went up in a good many of the branches whose output declined (see Appendix, Table 4.7).

3   During the period from May–July 1970 to the second quarter of 1971, demand for many industrial products again declined, yet the wholesale prices for the same products rose or remained unchanged; only a few prices fell or rose together with rising demand and output (see Appendix, Table 4.8).

Much the same developments occurred in the United States during the 1958 and 1970 recessions. In 1958 industrial production declined by 8 per cent, the degree of capacity utilisation fell by 9 points (from 82·3 to 73·6) and prices rose by 2 per cent; the corresponding figures for 1970 are −4·4 per cent, −7 points, and +3·9 per cent. The explanation, in my view, lies not in time lags or expectations, which can always be assumed more or less arbitrarily to suit the purposes of analysis, but quite simply in the movements of costs (labour cost and raw material prices). In other words, it was a cost inflation *not* accompanied by demand inflation, but on the contrary associated with − admittedly slight − demand deflation.

This sort of situation is nowadays called recession with inflation, or else stagflation, as the case may be. There is nothing paradoxical or extraordinary in it so long as one bears in mind that in industry demand changes as a rule give rise to changes not in prices but in output, within the limits of plant capacity, [15] and that price changes as a rule are a response to cost changes.

11 *Imported inflation*

While industry and retail trade are the characteristic playgrounds of cost inflation, and agriculture and mining those of demand inflation, imported inflation may hit any type of commodity − food or manufactures bought abroad, whether or not they compete with similar home-produced goods, or imported raw materials for the use of domestic industry. Some fundamental questions remain to be clarified. To do so, I recall the equation expressing the short-term variations on industrial prices in an open economy (see Chapter 2, section 15, note 23):

$$\dot{P}_i = \gamma \, \dot{L}_i + \delta \, \dot{M}_i + \eta \, \dot{P}_{iwo} \qquad (4.3)$$

This equation may serve to illustrate three questions, two of theory and one of fact. The first question has to do with the origin of international inflation. The second question is this: in what conditions do rising prices in industry cause profit margins to decrease? The third question concerns the relative intensity of domestic and international pressures on industrial wholesale prices in recent years in Italy.

Let us begin with the first question. Formally, we have to consider two of the three explanatory variables, namely, the index of raw material prices, M_i, and the index of world prices of manufactures, P_{iwo}. Generally speaking, the prices of agricultural raw materials and minerals vary in the short period with changes in demand and supply, provided production and sale take place in competitive conditions; in near-monopoly conditions, prices are altered by the producers at their discretion, in the light of the characteristics and expected changes of demand. In any given country the prices of industrial products, on the other hand, vary in the short term in response to changes in direct cost and in the prices of industrial goods produced in other countries. In recent years, both raw materials and the finished products of industry have been tending to go up in price, the former much more so than the latter. Why has this been so? What is the origin of this current international inflation?

Parts of the answer lie scattered here and there in previous chapters. Let us briefly recapitulate the relevant points, adding what may be necessary for fuller understanding.

1   At the root of our world-wide inflation lies the crisis of the international monetary system, and this in turn is largely due to what has been happening in the American economy. 'Excessive' expansion of public spending, especially for military purposes, has in itself generated very considerable inflationary pressure, and, together with the growing competitive strength of European countries and Japan, has led to an 'excessive' deficit in the US balance of payments. It is this deficit which is the direct cause of the chain reaction of currency devaluations, beginning with the dollar, and which has undermined the stability of the ruling dollar standard (see Chapter 2, Sections 10 and 12). The inflationary pressure generated by the international monetary crisis is driving up the prices of raw materials and manufactures alike.

2   Rapid and simultaneous economic growth in many countries, both capitalist and collectivist, has caused demand for raw materials to outpace supply, so that certain producers have come to enjoy a near-monopoly position. Consequently, commodity prices have been soaring (see Chapter 3, section 7, under the added impact of stockpiling – on the part of major companies for speculative reasons (in the expectation of further price rises), and on the part of some governments as a precaution against scarcities likely to impair military strength and/or growth prospects. (The explosion of raw material prices, which as a rule are quoted in dollars, started after August 1971, that is, after the dollar had ceased to be convertible into gold and, eventually, was devalued. Shortages of certain raw materials as a result of special circumstances were a contributory factor in that price explosion.)

3   International propagation of inflation is aided by the interaction of price increases through a mechanism schematically represented by the equation reproduced above.

As regards the second question, rising prices depress profit margins when international prices of manufactures remain stationary while raw material prices or labour cost, or both, go up. It is in such conditions that cost increases are usually, in part, shifted onto prices. When, on the contrary, international manufacturing prices go up while raw material prices and labour cost do not rise or rise proportionally less, then the restraining influence of foreign competition weakens and both domestic wholesale prices and profit margins rise.

The international price of manufactures can be pushed up artificially, by means either of a devaluation of the domestic currency, or of floating exchange rates if, in practice, they imply *de facto* devaluation. It is true that in such a case the prices of imported raw materials go up as well. But devaluation can be used, in the course of time, to raise domestic wholesale prices in the same proportion; and wholesale prices represent total *revenue* per unit of output, whereas raw material prices are only a part of *cost* per unit of output. Consequently, profits may go up even before the rate of price increase catches up with the rate of devaluation, provided only that, on the average, prices rise enough to exceed raw material costs. In any case, devaluation means an attempt to reduce the incidence of labour cost on revenue per unit of output; indirectly, devaluation means a reduction in the rate of increase, or in the level, of real wages. And this is likely to give rise to new economic and social tensions.

To answer the third question, we have to distinguish — in a first approximation and leaving the process of propagation aside — between the pressures of domestic and those of international origin which were at work in the inflation from which Italian industry suffered in recent years. To this end, I reproduce from Chapter 2 (note 23) the equation which 'explains' industrial wholesale price variations in terms of the main cost elements as well as of international prices for manufactures, with figures for the 'contribution' imputable to each of the explanatory variables:

$$\dot{P}_i = -0.066 + 0.299\,\dot{L}_i + 0.388\,\dot{M}_i + 0.463\,\dot{P}_{iwo}$$
$$t = (0.212)\ (4.253)\quad (5.011)\quad (2.964)$$

$$R^2 = 0.808 \qquad DW = 1.904$$

	$\dot{L}_i$			$\dot{M}_i$			$\dot{P}_{iwo}$			$\dot{P}_i$	
	(a)	(b)	(c)	(a)	(b)	(c)	(a)	(b)	(c)	actual	calculated
1968	2·5	0·7	....	1·1	0·4	....	−0·9	−0·4	....	0	0·7
1969	1·1	0·3	6%	8·0	3·1	60%	3·7	1·7	34%	3·5	5·1
1970	15·9	4·7	54%	3·0	1·2	14%	6·4	2·9	32%	8·7	8·8
1971	8·1	2·4	56%	1·0	0·3	7%	3·5	1·6	37%	4·1	4·3
1972	3·8	1·1	25%	4·0	1·6	36%	3·8	1·7	39%	3·9	4·4
1973*	12·0	3·6	19%	30·0	11·6	61%	8·0	3·7	20%		18·9

* Forecasts.

Explanation:
(a) Total variation per cent; (b) value of (a) multiplied by the coefficient in the equation; (c) explanatory contribution (per cent of the calculated value of $\dot{P}_i$). P_i stands for industrial prices, L_i for labour cost (ratio of hourly wages to output per man-hour), M_i for the prices of imported raw materials, and P_{iwo} for international industrial prices. The dots over the symbols indicate rates of change.

Prices were stable in 1968 and rose at varying, but always high, rates from then on. It seems that international price pressures were dominant in 1969 (60 + 34 = 94 per cent) and in 1972 (75 per cent), and that the same will happen in 1973 (81 per cent); domestic pressures (labour cost) were the main influence in 1970 (54 per cent) and in 1971 (56 per cent), but only just ahead of international ones.

All this is, of course, an altogether hypothetical exercise. However, if it is foolish to put one's trust in such exercises and to pretend that they are as good as empirical proof, it is not all that clever, either, to deny their usefulness *a priori*, provided they have a theoretical basis. Critical examination should then concentrate primarily on the theory behind these exercises.

In the equation and tabulation above, demand does not appear, for the simple reason that in the underlying theoretical model demand *normally, and in the aggregate*, is not relevant for an explanation of industrial price variations. The 'explanation' is satisfactory enough both in theoretical and in empirical terms, without introducing any indicators of demand pressure. However, demand is, in the same model, one of the explanatory factors for variations in the prices of agricultural commodities and raw materials. Monetary and credit policy affects wages via changes in investment, employment and unemployment, and, *in this indirect way*, also influences industrial wholesale prices. Hence monetary and credit policy has a bearing on prices in many different ways, but not in the simplistic way assumed in the theory of demand inflation. Anyone who is still inclined to use monetary policy to control wages would first have to disprove the objections here set out. Just because many different factors are in play, and because they may work in opposite directions, there is good reason for rejecting the argument that demand expansion is a necessary condition of price rises.

Due allowance made for the interaction of all the pressures at work, it may be said that in general monetary policy is more likely to push prices up when it is expansionary than when it is cautious. The same inquisitive spirit that led me to indulge in the hypothetical exercise discussed above, led me also to make another calculation. I worked out that, considering the prevailing level of resource utilisation in the four years 1964 to 1967, industrial investment could have fully returned to its 1963 level two years earlier than it actually did provided the increase in total liquidity and net security issues had been 5 to 10 per cent higher than it actually was. Such a monetary and credit policy might, via intricate interactions, have caused wages and prices to rise more, in average annual terms, than they actually did, but the additional increases would have been small (1 to 2 per cent in the case of wages, and 0·4 to 0·7 per cent in that of prices). And real income could have grown by at least one additional point per year (on the average by 5·8 instead of 4·8).

My sole purpose in discussing the results of my conjectures is to call forth more systematic and more thorough research. There can be no doubt that methodical simulation with well-constructed economic models is indispensable for better comprehension of the role of monetary policy and of the consequences of alternative choices.

12 *Concluding remarks*

An attempt has been made here to interpret the puzzling contrast in the behaviour of industrial investment and hourly productivity in Italy's industry during the last twenty years or so. From 1951 to 1963 both rose; from 1964 to 1969 productivity went on rising at much the same rate as before in the face of nil investment.

In looking for the reasons for the investment slump in 1964–65 and for the disappointing investment recovery in the following years, we have identified at least two: relatively low profits and (for the years 1964 to 1967) the investment behaviour of public enterprises. In addition, there is reason to believe that, after 1965, the public-sector deficit was holding back expansion and that its dampening effect was strengthened by the methods by which it was financed. To be precise, it must be added that this applies not to absolute levels, but to the rate of increase in investment and income; the restraining effect of the public-sector deficit was particularly serious in 1967.

The reason why the methods of financing the deficit added to its restrictive effect is, in my view, that the authorities underestimated the scope for monetary and credit expansion. It is true that, given the size of the public deficit after 1965, there was in any case bound to be a conflict between financing it and the requirements of the private sector, but the point is that this conflict could have been shifted to higher levels of real and financial flows.

To the extent that my criticisms are accepted as valid, they are addressed not only, and not even mainly, to the monetary authorities, including more especially the Bank of Italy, but to the government itself. With particular reference to the most recent years, it is the government which must be held responsible for more than once allowing the central bank to take on tasks which strictly speaking were not incumbent upon it, and also, on at least two important occasions, for having adopted the harmful expedient of putting off pressing decisions of general economic policy. For example, the government did very little to regulate short-term demand via the budget, even to the extent to which it would have been possible, and instead left the central bank to do what it could by credit policy. Furthermore, the persistence of the investment slump in 1965 could probably have been avoided and recovery speeded up if the government had acted more quickly to reflate demand, in the first place via public-enterprise investment. Then again, in 1967, when, as the Committee of Economic Advisers to the Government made clear as early as May 1966, conditions were favourable, nothing was done to step up public investment spending — with the consequence that later, in 1968, hasty measures had to be taken to raise public consumption spending (via a rise in pensions) at a time when it was obvious to all that demand reflation was needed and there was increasing pressure for revaluing the lira.

As regards changes in productivity and employment, these depend, generally speaking, not only on the volume of investment, but also on the type of investment and on reorganisation of the production process. The underlying principles of financial policy, especially with respect to security issues by the private sector, as well as the conspicuous increases in labour cost in the years 1962, 1963 and 1964, help to explain the movements of productivity and employment during the second of the two periods under consideration, that is, 1964 to 1969. At that point the discussion stops. I have deliberately left aside the most recent years, when circumstances were too special to warrant any conclusions.

It hardly needs stressing that the hypotheses underlying my interpretation of financial policy as well as of the course of productivity and employment are tentative. I cannot be certain that they are correct and have put them forward for the sole purpose of inducing others to test them and, if necessary, to amend them or indeed replace them by altogether different ones. But I am convinced of one thing, and this is that investment and productivity, on the one hand, and financial flows on the other, must be considered and explained simultaneously, so that we are not again landed with the analytical dichotomy between real and financial phenomena.

Postscript (October 1971): Comments on the role of public enterprises

The figures shown in Table 4.1 (Section 5 above) suggest that there was a policy switch with regard to public enterprises after 1967. Their investment fell year after year from 1964 to 1966, thus making the recession worse and impeding recovery; in 1967 it went up just a little, and thereafter a good deal more, so that in 1968 and 1969, and even more so in 1970 and 1971, public-enterprise investment was the very mainstay of overall investment growth in industry (excluding building).

Taking up the classification of industrial investment by source from where we left it in Table 4.1, Table 4.1a shows what happened from 1967 onward. (The figures for 1971 were modified and those for 1972 were added in November 1973.)

Table 4.1a

Industrial investment at constant prices, 1967 to 1972
(rates of change, per cent)

| Year | Public enterprises | | Private enterprises | Total |
	State-controlled	Total		
1967	+ 0·8	+ 7·1	+ 16·3	+ 13·1
1968	+ 14·2	+ 11·1	+ 10·4	+ 10·7
1969	+ 24·9	+ 16·8	+ 5·0	+ 11·0
1970	+ 19·2	+ 17·8	+ 7·5	+ 12·8
1971	+ 32·6	+ 21·9	− 17·0	0
1972	+ 10·0	+ 4·0	− 9·6	− 2·8

It is striking to see public enterprises spending so much more on investment in the latest two years at a time when private investment in industry came to halt and then fell off.

It certainly does look as though the government's policy regarding industrial investment by public enterprises changed very radically after 1967, though it is not known whether this was by deliberate design. Before then, the government's attitude can only be described as hostile, no doubt under pressure from the large private concerns which regarded public enterprises as dangerous competitors, not least in institutional terms. The idea was to stop public enterprise from growing any further, to keep it out of industry and step up public investment only in 'infrastructural services, more especially in transport and communications, and in rationalisation schemes in the areas complementary to agricultural activities'. This was the place marked out for public enterprise, including state-controlled companies. We read further: 'There is no case, on the other hand, for trying to raise the level of public investment by venturing any

152

further into other sectors, including especially manufacturing industry. All that would happen is that government-controlled companies would compete with private entrepreneurs and would so upset the very base of their economic calculations that the effects are hard to foretell.'

Actually, public-enterprise investment was less hamstrung in the southern regions, but even there a cautious approach prevailed.

The two quotations above are from the Concluding Remarks made by the Governor of the Bank of Italy at the shareholders' meeting in May 1966. [16] Nothing and nobody could express the dominating view more effectively. Here we certainly have one explanation for the disconcerting investment behaviour of public enterprises in the years 1964 to 1967, as described in section 5 of this chapter.

After 1967 Italy's economic policy-makers changed their attitude – witness the figures in Tables 4.1 and 4.1a, as well as a stream of news items about takeovers, mergers and agreements involving state-controlled and private concerns, not to speak of a growing number of rescue operations. Private industrial enterprise repeatedly got into serious difficulties – witness the behaviour of the share of profits in the gross product of manufacturing industry (see Table 4.2 in Section 6 above, and also Table 3.2 in the Appendix to Chapter 3) – mainly as a result of the surge of wages which in 1962–1963, and again later in 1970–1971, assumed almost explosive proportions. In any event, wages were racing ahead of productivity, which in turn was increasing a good deal more slowly than before, mainly under the impact of more and more frequent labour disputes. The unions at that time were pressing not only wage claims, but also – and in some cases, mainly – demands for better working conditions on the factory floor (limitation of work in 'unsocial hours', rules for job assignments, prevention of accidents, healthy surroundings, etc.) They also wanted to see the reform programme get under way. To talk to management about such broader aims, and if necessary to strike for them, bears witness to the workers' growing civic maturity, since it shows that they are no longer concerned merely with their pay packet and no longer passively accept their subordinate status. But this socially welcome development is economically costly, at least in the short run. In Italy, it has probably done very much to create the difficulties with which so many firms have to contend today.

Of course growing union militancy is not peculiar to Italy. The same has been happening in recent years in France, Great Britain and Western Germany, in formerly untroubled Sweden, and also in the United States. In all industrial countries distinctly more hours are lost through strikes at times when inflation gathers speed and assumes international character, as happened during the Korean war, the early sixties and again now since 1969.

But in Italy labour conflicts are nearly always more bitter than elsewhere. The workers' aims are broader, too, since Italian unions, more than those elsewhere, are intent on political influence and in particular want to see some of the reforms they have been advocating. As you make your bed, so you must lie on it. Ever since the end of the war the ruling classes have been procrastinating, putting things off, even though paying lip service to the need for radical institutional and structural change. Social tension mounted and finally erupted. Private enterprise has never been soundly based in Italy. After the war many companies became bigger and in some respects stronger, but at once they were up against growing trade union pressure and international competition. Here we have the real reasons for the policy turnabout which I mentioned: the only alternative to increasing government intervention in industrial production was − and is − stagnation of output or an economic depression far worse than the one that ushered in the seventies. [17] As more and more firms have been getting into difficulties, public agencies had to step in more often with a variety of rescue operations; more and more mergers have been arranged; and foreign groups have seen their chance to buy whole companies on the cheap. Indeed, not the least of the purposes of official encouragement of rescue operations by public firms has been to keep foreign takeovers at bay; after all, as between public and foreign ownership, the former seemed the lesser evil.

Symbiosis of private and public capital has long been characteristic of Italian industry. Public capital has been gaining ground in recent years and will most probably continue to do so, though perhaps discontinuously. All this raises new problems both of analysis and policy. There is fairly general agreement among economic experts today that the chief determinants of industrial investment are demand, the capital stock, the profit rate (as an incentive), total profits (as a source of self-financing), and the increase in total liquidity (as an indicator of the supply of outside finance funds). Strictly speaking, these determinants are relevant only for industrial investment by private firms. For public enterprise the chief determinants are not necessarily the same, or at least the parameters are presumably different. For instance, it is likely that profit counts for less (both as an investment incentive and as a source of self-financing), and rather than total liquidity, the best indicators of the supply of external finance funds are perhaps bond issues by the public sector in industry as well as endowment fund increases (during the period when they are actually paid out). [18] Finally, one has to take account of large-scale investment projects which are decided on by the government in agreement with the management of public industrial concerns and the profitability of which is not always assured at the moment of decision. [19]

In any event, it must be assumed that in Italy, at least since 1968, less trust can be put in the interpretative power of one single equation for the statistical 'explanation' of aggregate industrial investment, even in a first approximation. At least two equations are needed, one for private investment and one for public-enterprise investment.

The second set of new analytical problems is the concern of sociologists and political scientists. It is up to them to identify the meaning and consequences of the current evolution and of its possible outcome. In the most general terms, one can foresee two possibilities. One of them is that Italy will move towards a socialist type of economy, with more and more of the means of production effectively in public ownership, and with growing political control and growing 'dialectical' participation [20] of workers and technicians in the powers of decision so far the prerogative of small groups of industrialists and managers. The alternative seems to be a system in which combined economic power and political power increasingly accumulates in the hands of a limited circle of private and 'public' top-level executives in close contact with each other. This would amount to oligarchic management of the economy, largely withdrawn from effective public control, and no doubt riddled with increasingly scandalous forms of corruption and patronage. Personally, I would regard the first development as natural and sound, and the second as pathological; but as things are today, there are as many pointers in one direction as in the other — more, if anything, in the second direction. But the future is still wide open. It will depend on the strategy of political parties, especially those which claim to be on the left, and of trade unions, and on the choices of their leaders and of the country's intellectuals.

I said a little while ago that the faster pace of wage rises and, more generally, growing union militancy were not peculiar to Italy, but common to most industrial countries. The same can be said of the ensuing fall in profits. As an example, Table 4.6 shows the share of profits (net of depreciation and general expenses) in the national income of United Kingdom. [21]

It seems that the profit share fell even more sharply in the United Kingdom than it did in Italy (cf. Table 3.2 in the Appendix to Chapter 3), though it must be noted that the Italian figures refer to all firms in manufacturing industry, and to profits before deduction of depreciation, whereas the British figures refer to the company sector of all branches and to profits after deduction of depreciation. But the point of interest here is

155

Table 4.6

Profits/income ratio in the United Kingdom, 1950 to 1970

1950–54	25·2	1966	17·6
1955–59	22·8	1967	18·1
1960–64	21·0	1968	16·8
1964	21·2	1969	14·2
1965	20·2	1970	12·0*

* Provisional estimate.

the tendency, and there can be no doubt that the profit share did fall both in Italy and in Great Britain, and that it fell sharply. Figures published recently by the Organisation for Economic Co-operation and Development [22] on the income share of wage earners suggest that the profit share has likewise been falling, though less steeply, in other industrial countries (including the United States and Canada), especially during the last five or six years.

The question arises of how to distinguish between what is common to the majority of industrial countries and what is peculiar to Italy. First of all the fall in the profit share was steeper in Italy than in most other countries, though it was conspicuous in the United Kingdom too. But the main difference is that in Italy we have had for many years a very large sector of state-controlled companies, which now, because of the difficulties afflicting private enterprise, is expanding even further, both via existing groups and via new ones, like GEPI (*Gestioni e partecipazioni industriali*). [23] There are other countries, like Great Britain, which have large public concerns, and yet others, like the United States, where public intervention in industry takes place on the side of demand rather than supply, in the sense that many large concerns rely heavily on government orders. In both these countries the government has recently had to step in more and more frequently to salvage ailing companies (the recent affairs of the Pennsylvania Railroad, Chrysler and Rolls Royce are merely the most eye-catching cases). But the situation in Italy is still specifically different, and in present circumstances it would seem that the comparison does not work altogether to Italy's disadvantage. After all, in some countries, like England and Sweden, consideration is now being given to the expediency of 'importing' the Italian system of state equity holdings — probably for the very purpose of using it as a prop for the system of private enterprise. In any case, these structural differences merely underline the similarity of the problems which have to be dealt with and which, in the last analysis, were thrown up by the wave of claims, regarding wages and other matters, advanced by the trade unions and the labour movement.

They are very serious problems, so much so that, at present, they are holding back economic growth and augmenting unemployment. There is no comfort for Italy in the thought that other countries have the same sort of problems in different form, and of different intensity; nor is there any room for complacency. We must never forget the specific responsibilities that fall upon politicians, union leaders and — private and public — management alike. But the very fact that these problems are common to many countries may help us to look at them in constructive terms, rather than simply to put the blame on conflicts among the coalition parties, or on the short-sightedness of politicians or yet on the mistakes of trade unions. All these things do exist, and they deserve to be denounced and criticised; but the problems are so grave just because their origin lies much deeper. Italian industry really is in a structural crisis, which is not as yet fully understood.

Post-postscript (December 1973)

After two years of recession (1970–71) and almost a year of stagnation, the Italian economy entered a stage of recovery late in 1972. In the first half of 1973 this was aided, in Italy, by the *de facto* devaluation of the lira against major currencies (cf. Section 11 above); later, control of certain prices and moderate credit restriction created difficulties, without, however, jeopardising recovery at least in the short run. A much more serious threat to recovery and growth is now coming from the energy crisis which has been precipitated by the policy of the Arab countries and of the leading multinational oil companies, and which is hitting all Europe's economies, in different degree but certainly much more seriously than the American economy.

But petroleum is only a special case, though probably the most important, of a much more general problem which at present is the chief source of inflation in the industrialised capitalist countries. I have in mind the problem of the scarcity of many raw materials, which is likely to reappear again and again in the future with increasing intensity (cf. Chapter 3, Section 7). Inflation originating mainly in rising raw material prices is a perverse sort of inflation, in the sense that it does not favour but impedes growth, for two reasons: first, because it causes industrial costs to rise faster than the prices of finished products, with a consequent fall in

157

profits (which can only temporarily be offset by devaluation – see Section 11 above), and secondly because it leads to increasing balance-of-payments difficulties. In any case, the energy crisis heralds a very difficult period for all European countries and particularly for Italy, where it piles new troubles upon old ones.

Notes

[1] The figures for investment and capital per worker refer to industry, those for hourly productivity and output to manufacturing industry (lack of data made it impossible to consider manufacturing industry in all cases). The rates of change are my estimates on the basis of statistics published by the Central Statistical Institute, the Business Cycle Research Institute and the Ministry of Labour, except for the figures on capital per worker; these were calculated and kindly made available to me by Professor Onorato Castellino, to whom I am indebted also for critical suggestions which led me to revise section 3 and, on one point, section 8.

[2] For a balanced critical judgement of this policy choice, it must be recalled that the alternative to outright nationalisation would have been to hand the electricity industry over to an autonomous government-controlled corporation like IRI; this would have had much less unfavourable immediate effects, but seemed inadvisable in the light of the somewhat passive and feeble management of those electricity companies already belonging to the IRI Group (*Finelettrica*).

[3] After nationalisation, the bond market had, in addition, to digest conspicuous issues floated by the new National Electricity Board (ENEL), which needed investment funds at a time when profit margins, and hence self-financing, had dropped to very low levels in the electricity industry, for reasons which nobody had foreseen before nationalisation. Until then, the electricity industry was divided, some of it being in private and some in public hands, partly under government and partly under local authority control. Accordingly, there were wide differentials in wages and salaries. Nationalisation, that is, unified control of the whole industry, necessarily required wage and salary scales to be unified as well, and inevitably at the highest existing levels. These were in some cases very high indeed, because some companies, especially municipal ones, had shifted onto wage and salary increases some part of their monopoly profits, for which there were no other investment opportunities. This is a lesson which should be remembered every time plans are made for the nationalisation of any

branch of economic activity. (A similar problem is arising in Italy now, in connection with the reform of health services.)

[4] In terms of annual averages, a direct correlation can be seen between share prices and the profit share in industry; the correlation improves when alongside the profit share, the rate of change in total liquidity and US equity prices are included among the explanatory variables. (See Chapter 1, Section 17, and note 56.)

[5] See for instance the Annual Report of the Ministry of State Participations for 1968, p. 70.

[6] In the national accounts, investment by state-controlled enterprises is included in the 'private sector', as against public administration in the 'public sector'.

[7] As a point of possible interest, I reproduce the estimated equation for the period 1951–1968:

$$UN = 13 \cdot 757 - 0 \cdot 341\,\dot{R} - 0 \cdot 153\,\dot{I} - 0 \cdot 103\,\dot{E}_i + 0 \cdot 189\,Z$$
$$t = (13 \cdot 875)\ (4 \cdot 629)\quad (7 \cdot 072)\quad (4 \cdot 313)\quad (3 \cdot 146) \qquad (4.4)$$

$$R^2 = 0 \cdot 937 \qquad\qquad DW = 1 \cdot 701$$

where UN is the degree of unused capacity, R is dependent labour income (whose changes are assumed to be representative of those in private consumption), I stands for industrial investment, E_i for industrial exports and Z for the public borrowing requirement (cf. Italian national accounts in the supplement to the Monthly Statistical Bulletin, January 1970); for all the coefficients t is significant at the level of 99 per cent; dots over symbols denote rates of change.

The result cannot out of hand be interpreted as meaning that an increase in the public debt raises the degree of unused capacity; it can be argued that cause and effect are the other way round — that is, that an increase in the degree of unused capacity, which in turn is a consequence of a decline in the gross national product, causes the budget deficit and, with it, the public debt, to increase to the extent that tax revenue falls while public expenditure remains unchanged.

In my view, two influences are simultaneously at work: the one just mentioned and the one discussed in the next, to wit, that, other things being equal, an increase in the public debt reduces the chances of private borrowing and hence reduces total private investment in non-agricultural sectors (agricultural investment is heavily subsidised and therefore largely unaffected by these influences). To test this hypothesis, I calculated another equation in addition to the one reproduced above, which, for the sake of keeping my model simple, includes only industrial investment

159

instead of total non-agricultural investment. In the following equation total non-agricultural investment replaces industrial investment:

$$UN = 17 \cdot 922 - 0 \cdot 469 \, \dot{R} - 0 \cdot 136 \, \dot{E}_i - 0 \cdot 312 \, \dot{I}_t$$
$$t = (21 \cdot 223) \quad (6 \cdot 835) \quad (5 \cdot 022) \quad (7 \cdot 707) \qquad (4.5)$$
$$R^2 = 0 \cdot 917 \qquad\qquad DW = 1 \cdot 456$$

The correlation is virtually as good as with equation (4.4), and certainly much better than when the public debt is excluded from an equation taking account of industrial investment alone. This indicates that public borrowing takes the place of such non-agricultural investment as is not included in industrial investment; it follows that there is some inverse correlation between total non-agricultural investment and the public debt. And indeed the coefficient of simple correlation between the two, while low, is negative: it equals $-0 \cdot 440$.

(The lines of reasoning followed in working out the unused capacity equation of the updated model in the Postscript to Chapter 1 and that followed here are not mutually incompatible, so that the industrial investment variable with a two-year lag, $I_{\tau - 2}$, used in the updated model and the public debt variable, Z, in the above equation (4.4) could be used together, in addition to the three basic explanatory variables common to the two equations – R, I and E_i; alternatively, the lagged investment variable could be added in the above equation (4.5). These variants are not presented, merely for the sake of simplicity.)

[8] Banca d'Italia, *Abridged Version of the Report for the Year 1969*, Rome 1970, p. 96.

[9] The question of the relationships between increase in the monetary base, expansion of the money supply, net bond issues and bond prices is as complicated as it is important. To elucidate these relationships needs econometric analysis, which, as Dr Tommaso Padoa Schioppa has pointed out to me, should take account also of non-financial assets.

[10] It should be added that in 1967 the restrictive influence of the budget was especially severe, not only because the deficit shrank (by some 600 billion lire), but because of the methods by which this reduction was brought about. What happened was that firms were again made to pay certain social charges previously shouldered by the state. As a result profit margins, which were just picking up a little, were again squeezed, much to the detriment of investment and economic growth.

[11] Cf. G. La Malfa and S. Vinci, 'Il saggio di partecipazione delle forze di lavoro in Italia' *L'Industria* no. 4, 1970.

[12] This argument seems to fit in with the neo-classical theory of the

substitutability of factors of production, especially capital and labour, in response to relative factor prices. This is not the place to go into this intricate question, but it may just be pointed out that neo-classical theory is concerned with factor substitutability in static terms, whereas here the argument is entirely set in a dynamic context; on the other hand, the substitution between labour and specific capital goods (not 'capital') takes place only under particular conditions. See my paper 'Technical Progress, Prices and Growth: An Introduction', in a volume to be published by the University of Campinas, Brazil.

[13] There is no doubt that after the 1964 recession firms went in much more for internal rationalisation, and that this, with the tougher working schedules it entailed, contributed to the workers' resentments which eventually erupted in the 'hot autumn' of 1969.

[14] See Chapter 2, Section 7.

[15] See my *Oligopoly and Technical Progress*, Harvard University Press, revised edition, 1969, p. 73n., 84–5, 168.

[16] Banca d'Italia, *Abridged Version of the Report for the Year 1965*, Rome 1966, p. 144.

[17] I agree with Sergio Vaccà in regarding the current crisis as a 'structural' one, and I also agree with his diagnosis, which has much in common with my own. In examining the reasons for the rapid expansion of the public sector in industry Vaccà rightly mentions, in addition to falling profits, the direct and indirect effects of the nationalisation of the electricity industry, which was one of the pillars of private industrial enterprise, as well as the unhealthy growth of speculative property investment for the sake of the rent of urban sites. See S. Vaccà, 'Crisi strutturale e non solo crisi ciclica – Prime considerazioni per una strategia industriale' *Mondo economico*, 23 October 1971.

[18] Appropriations to endowment funds fall under the heading of capital transfers from the state to firms. But it is a mistake to think that these transfers go wholly, or even mainly, to public enterprises. Private companies, especially large ones, likewise receive transfers in the form of subsidies, equity capital, tax exemptions and various special credit facilities, including export credits.

[19] Cases in point are the steel complex at Taranto, the Alfasud motor car factory, the chemical works in Sardinia and the desalination plant at Gela. The desalination plant at Gela is an example of an investment not subject to market forces, yet not for this reason unsound; the desalted water is to be purchased from the company concerned at remunerative prices and sold at a political price, the difference to be covered by taxes.

[20] By dialectical participation I mean a system of organisation and

decision-making in which both management and workers retain their independence. One might think of arrangements, for example, under which management works out investment projects and then discusses major ones with workers' committees, who would have the right to suggest changes or to put forward alternative projects; management would be under an obligation to review the original projects in the light of these suggestions, and, in case of disagreement not otherwise resolved, the final decision would rest with the planning authorities. This is of course merely a working hypothesis, which needs to be examined closely and fully discussed; but it does go to show how far we have yet to go in devising effective and not merely palliative forms of worker participation in industry.

[21] A. Glyn and B. Sutcliffe, 'The Critical Condition of British Capital' *New Left Review* no. 6, 1970, Table A.

[22] OECD, *Inflation: The Present Problem. Report by the Secretary General*, Paris 1970, Part II, C.

[23] Perhaps it is no exaggeration to suggest that the current rapid expansion of the economic area covered by state-controlled companies is, from the quantitative point of view, comparable with that which took place during the Great Depression, from 1933 to 1940. However, qualitatively speaking, the great change occurred precisely in 1933, with the creation of IRI, the Industrial Reorganisation Institute. It is of some interest to recall that the formula for a company with equity holdings in state hands was originally proposed by two liberal economists, Luigi Einaudi and Pasquale Jannaccone, during the first world war — the idea being to speed up the development of the armaments industry. See Vittorio Foa's Introduction to the second edition of P. Grifone, *Il capitale finanziario in Italia*, Einaudi, Turin 1971, p. xlii—xliii.

Appendix

Table 4.7

Industrial output and prices in the 1963–1965 recession[a].
Changes in three-month averages from September–November 1963
to the first quarter of 1965 (per cent)

		Changes in	
		output	prices
Overall index		− 5·4	+ 2·3
1	Glass	− 3·1	+ 6·1
2	Transport equipment	− 18·3	+ 6·0
3	Textile industry: fabrics	− 38·6	+ 5·7
4	Hides and leather	− 24·7	+ 5·0
5	Food industry	− 19·4	+ 4·8
6	Rubber	− 11·2	+ 3·8
7	Iron and steel industry: tubes	− 15·9	+ 3·5
8	Engineering: non-electric machinery	− 18·3	+ 2·3
9	Engineering: electric machinery	− 32·7	− 0·8
10	Paper	− 12·1	− 5·2
11	Cement	− 32·7	− 5·1
12	Wood	− 10·2	− 5·8
13	Iron and steel industry: sheets	+ 32·4	− 2·2
14	Petroleum derivatives	+ 33·8	+ 1·7
15	Chemicals	+ 5·6	+ 6·5

a   Seasonal variations are eliminated by using three-month averages −
perhaps the least arbitrary method.

Source: Monthly Statistical Bulletin of the Central Statistical Institute.

Table 4.8

Industrial output and prices in the 1970–1971 recession[a, b, c]
Changes in three-month averages from May-July 1970
to the second quarter of 1971 (per cent)

		Changes in output	Changes in prices
Overall index		− 4·3	+ 2·8
1	Cement	− 7·8	+ 4·2
2	Electric cables	− 4·2	+ 11·0
3	Fuel oil	− 1·3	+ 19·6
4	Leather	− 7·2	+ 4·9
5	Footwear	− 0·2	+ 10·1
6	Processed and preserved meat	− 5·4	+ 2·1
7	Sulphuric acid	− 4·9	0
8	Lubricating oil	− 8·4	0
9	Newsprint	− 10·1	0
10	Cotton fabrics	− 16·7	0
11	Cotton yarns	− 24·7	− 8·1
12	Aluminium	− 14·6	− 1·2
13	Sheet and plate glass	+ 14·4	0
14	Biscuits	+ 6·4	0
15	Tyres	+ 7·4	+ 7·8

a   See note to Table 4.7.

b   The categories of goods in Tables 4.7 and 4.8 are not the same, because in the interval the Central Statistical Institute changed its industry classification. The products actually included have been chosen in the light of the availability of the most comparable figures. The output figures are national averages, but prices are different in different markets, and an effort was made to select identical or, at least, very similar products.

c   As of September 1971, the latest analytical figures at hand were those of June 1971; it was for this reason, and not because the recession had touched bottom, that the three months April–June 1971 were chosen as the second term of the comparison. In the preceding boom, the production index reached its peak in October 1970; since the three months August–October seemed unsuitable for purposes of comparison, because of the habitual distortions of output in August, there remained the choice between September—November or May—July 1970. The latter three months promised the more comparable figures, because two thirds of the period coincide with the 1971 period. Actually, the results are much the same in both cases.

Source: Monthly Statistical Bulletin of the Central Statistical Institute.

Index

Value productivity and wages 90, 95–6
'Verdoorn's Law' 43–4; *see also* Investment; Productivity

Wage differentials 16, 17, 44, 58n54; drift 15, 53n12; equations 16, 36, 74, 90–2, 104n24, 104n25
Wage-price policy, *see* Incomes policy
Wage-price spiral 40, 81, 114
Wages: and investment 14, 39, 43; and marginal analysis 14, 52n10; determinants of 17–20, 36, 46, 74, 97–9; limits to the variations of 14–17, 81; long-run variations 90, 92–4; optimum rate of increase in 20–4; short-run variations 15–16, 58n54, 74–6, 90–2, 104n24, 104n25; wages bill and liquidity 13; *see also* Cost of living; Labour-saving innovations; Productivity; Profits; Trade unions; Unemployment; Value productivity

DATE DUE

DEC 0 1 1979			
OCT 1 0 1989			
OCT 1 7 1989			

UPI

Printed
in USA